EVOLVE

A GUIDEBOOK TO INTENTIONAL LIVING

MORGAN THORN GREY,
LCPC. ExAT. ENERGIST

Published by the Unapologetic Voice House
www.theunapologeticvoicehouse.com
Scottsdale, AZ.
Paperback ISBN: 978-1-955090-27-8
E-book ISBN: 978-1-955090-28-5
Library of Congress Control Number: 2022909719
Cover designer: Marie Stirk
Edited by: Jessica Wolf

This book is in acknowledgment to my children who have helped me learn and grow and continue to inspire me along this path of life.

And to my wife who will follow me anywhere with encouragement "...just around the next corner"

TABLE OF CONTENTS

WELCOME TO YOUR WORKBOOK

A S A THERAPIST, I PLAY THE ROLE OF ADVISOR, GUIDE AND healer. It is both my passion and responsibility to pass along my knowledge. This passion comes not only from my education but what I have discovered working with my clients that resulted in empowering them to find their own passion and to live their best life.

The idea for this workbook came to me one day in a session with a client as she spoke about a book she was reading that was very meaningful to her. As she spoke, I could see how the author's experience seemed to weave together with what the reader learned and what my client then did to grow from these experiences. It made me realize how *my* collective experiences have given me the wisdom and ability to be the compassionate healer that I am today.

In life we all experience times of anger, sadness, loss, continued frustration, feelings of overwhelm, anxiety, shame, regret, loneliness, addiction, joy, gratefulness, miracles, hope, lov and yes—even suicidal ideation. As a behavioral scientist I wanted to figure out what all these emotions and experiences mean. I wanted to break it down and create a formula that can guide us all to a better way of living.

When I was in third grade I attended a birthday party in which we had a guest appearance by none other than the Fairy Godmother. We were each allowed one secret wish that we whispered into the Fairy Godmother's ear. She then handed us a typed-up response on a fortune-cookie sized piece of paper. Mine said, "You do not wish for raiment and such, you will get your wish my dear, for you do not ask for much." My wish was to be happy. I was nine-years old, and I carried this paper in my wallet well into my 20s until I lost it (or I lost hope of ever finding it). As I think back to my nine-year-old self, this wish seems pretty deep. My pursuit of the illusive "Happiness" has provided me with a lot of help along my way. As May West would say (and I would quote her often, usually after I realized the latest stupid thing I just survived didn't literally kill me) "I've always relied on the kindness of strangers." And indeed, I relied on others to either fill me up or tear me down. These people and my experiences have shaped my philosophy and my work I do today. In the end, my pursuit of happiness was realized in the small steps I've made to reclaim and take charge of my life. Instead of relying on the kindness of others, I have come to rely on myself.

This all started with a painfully slow realization. I create my world with my thoughts. I create what those thoughts are and I am in charge of how to change them. It is in the discovering of the what and the how around that reality that my philosophy unfolds.

I'm glad you have found yourself here.

Whether you picked this book up to help decrease stress, increase awareness, gain clarity about a new direction, to quit a habit, seize control over your seemingly chaotic life, understand yourself or your relationships, make sense of the challenges our planet and everyone on it is facing, or just feel better and live a happy, empowered and content life, this book will walk you through how to become more aware and ultimately live the life you were meant to live.

This workbook lays out my approach in therapy and is a blend of psychology, spirituality, and science. May aim is to craft this in a way that makes it easy for you to understand, learn and apply to your own life.

While those are lofty goals, rest assured we will "walk before we run" into saving the planet.

We will start with you.

As you go through this workbook my intention for you is to experience an increased awareness of your thoughts, your emotions and your behaviors. As you work through this book, I would like you to learn how you create your world and how you can change your world. My hope is that you will gain new perspectives, see new beginnings and begin to imagine and create the world you want to live in. Today you can begin your transformative, intentional life. You are the pebble dropped into the pond on this earth and just like the ripples moving out on that pond, you will soon see how working on yourself not only affects you but affects those around you. You are the healer. And, as you continue your journey of mastering the Laws of the Universe for yourself, you will positively affect your family, your friends, your communities and for the planet.

You are taking a brave step today—a commitment of sorts—and I am honored that you are going with me. I am always available for a consultation throughout your journey. You can reach me online at TheArtofLivingStudio.com. I look forward to hearing from you.

MORGAN'S EDUCATION

I have always considered myself an artist and graduated with a degree in visual communications and illustration from the University of Kansas. When I received my Masters Degree in Community Counseling from the University of Phoenix, I knew I needed to further my counseling education into the artistic field and so I also completed graduate studies in Expressive Arts Therapy from the I.S.I.S. Southwest (International School of Intermodal Studies). As my understanding expanded of how energy impacts our lives I became a certified Integrative Quantum Medicine ™ Practitioner and Teacher.

CHAPTER 1:

THE PHILOSOPHY BEHIND INTENTIONAL LIVING

Y APPROACH TO INTENTIONAL LIVING BLENDS PSYCHOL-ogy, spirituality/energy and science. In my career as a licensed therapist and expressive art therapist I began work in the nonprofit sector. I have had the privilege to work in many mental and behavioral health settings from outpatient, residential treatment, group homes, domestic violence and homeless shelters to private practice bringing into every scenario the expressive arts as a form of healing. All of these venues also provided me the privilege to work with many types of people, all seeking the same thing—understanding, healing and purpose. I have worked with clients alongside volunteers, supervisees, interns, and teams of other clinicians. While working with and among all these communities, I continued my focus on finding the formula, the truth, the answer, to the question that was in my mind as well as theirs—**how do humans get through the traumas, woundings, disappointments and setbacks of life and into a place of**

happiness? The intention of this workbook is to a help you find that formula, that truth, that path forward..

With this endgame in mind, I looked at the intersectionality of the energy healing of meditation, chakras, I Ching, expressive arts, and the science of epigenetics, as well as behavioral health science. I began teaching my clients how to meditate, sit in a drum circle, paint, sculpt, move their bodies, move through yoga asanas using the chakras to heal energetically and to tune into the messages of their bodies. I continued my study and found Louise Mita, founder and developer of Integrated Quantum Medicine,™ or IQM (www.taoenergy.com). IQM is a form of energy healing that combines traditional Chinese medicine and quantum theory. I began studying IQM in 2014 and I am an authorized Certified Practitioner and Teacher of IQM. As it turns out, it is the element that ties all my efforts into a final result of perfect health.

THE WEAVING TOGETHER OF THE THREE

PSYCHOLOGY

The psychology part of my work obviously comes from my foundational and continuing education in counseling, theory, interventions and practices. I particularly ascribe to concepts like Carl Rogers' unconditional positive regard which involves showing complete support and acceptance of a person no matter what that person says or does which recognizes that we are all looking for to be loved and accepted without judgment. And I give a nod to Jungian archetypes and the rich, complexes, subpersonalities, and the process of their integration. Using Expressive Arts Therapy a theory that combines all the arts—visual, written, sound, movement and drama—allowing for the a full body, metaphorical process to shift the psyche to crystallization—the ah-ha moment of clarity surrounding a disease. I use more clinically foundational interventions of cognitive behavioral therapy techniques, and my work in crisis honed my skills with brief solution-focused therapy strategies for accurate assessment of a client's area of concern. Motivational counseling skills help me guide clients skillfully to quick resolution. I studied extensively on what is called Reactive Attachment Disorder, which includes the spectrum of the development stages of attachment, abandonment, loss, grief, and trauma. My internship with a hospice agency allowed me to work with the grieving and the dying. My skills and knowledge deepened as I worked with clients experiencing symptoms of ADHD, anxiety and depression. My work with children and their families allowed me extensive practice in parenting, family dynamics and couple's therapy. All of these identified concerns weave into each other at times and overlap, calling for skilled discernment. I have learned to stand bravely, asking the tough questions, shining light on the unseen places of the psyche.

SPIRITUALITY (ENERGY)

The spirituality/energy part of my work is my foundation. I was always a thoughtful child, observing and watching. Pretending to sleep when I was really thinking. The concrete aspects of spirituality came to me in the form of organized religion. I was raised Presbyterian. We mostly only attended events and activities involving the church. Whether it was attending Sunday services, a potluck, softball game or campout, it was always through the church. I remember hearing messages about sinning and questioning the validity of this concept. I also remember staying up late and waking up before dawn at church camp waiting for a miracle to occur. Waiting for or a feeling of inspiration, an epiphany or a sign that Jesus or God was there. The more abstract concepts of spirituality came later in my life as I watched my mom, who had taught me to love everyone and everything unconditionally, become challenged my coming out as gay. She rejected me.

Who was this God that the structures of religion worshiped? I could no longer say "God" without feeling the pain of that rejection and I moved into claiming my right as a human to have a spiritual life. The Universe, energy and higher power, were resulting concepts I began to explore. Indeed, this is how I reconciled unconditional regard for all others and the ability to understand my clients who came to me with their unique spiritual beliefs and practices. This also brought me to a greater understanding that God was energy and we were swimming in it. Up until now, I felt my way in the world and often took on other people's thoughts and feelings as my own, only realizing later that I was saying and doing what others wanted, thinking it was me! I realized I was an empath, an intuitive and would often say "I don't have an original thought." I would tap into the higher energy fields of the Universe/God in order to create change. Without knowing I tapped into this skill with my clients who would often exclaim, "How did you know that?" When I studied expressive arts therapy my world opened a bit more and I saw the power of creating in a whole new way of giving a voice to the illusive parts of ourselves: feelings, emotions, thoughts and behaviors. expressive arts therapy stands apart from art therapy or music therapy in that it takes all the creative modalities into an interplay towards a deeper understanding for the client. It also states that being creative is for everyone and is necessary for the human experience.

It was through exploring spirituality that I was led into the field of energy work. Asking who God was led me to the science of God. And yes, scientists have proven that there is a God. E=MC2. Until Einstein formalized the relationship of mass energy, humans thought that matter was not a form of energy. Matter and Energy were thought of as two different entities. Einstein shows that matter is a condensed form of energy. The Conservation of Energy Law shows that energy can be converted from one form to another. God is energy based on this premise and made of matter and spirit or consciousness. Without spirit or consciousness, the human being is just matter. In fact, some believe that religion began based on science. Sadly, now it seems that religion has an inverse relationship with spirituality. Though labeled as "New Age" at the time, learning about meditation, chakras and energy fields, practices such as tarot reading, angel cards, The I Ching and even studying how the expressive arts create a shift, my perspective took a huge paradigm shift. Knowing our thoughts can alter situations —I began there. Once I discovered IQM and applied it to myself and my world, did I truly step into complete understanding of the laws of the universe and the energy that surrounds us.

SCIENCE

The science part of my work includes the exciting research of epigenetics. The behavioral and spiritual work that I did with my clients was supported by science. Through this process my holistic view of the human experience fell into place like the inner workings of a clock. The exciting bottom line is that researchers have identified the protein on the gene in the DNA that receives a signal from the environment and creates a pattern of response. This occurs all the time but most frequently from as early as four months into the womb up to six years old. This is how we learn to walk and talk and eat AND respond with and to emotions and to our world. We learn this response so well it becomes a subconscious reaction and feels like it is a piece of our personality. But epigenesists have found a reverse gene and learned that our reactions aren't determined. And that is what is so exciting. We learned from all the experiences and people who were around us at this age. The patterns we created can be set aside and new ones can be created. This means that our lives are not genetically determined, and they are a choice.

The custom-made patterns that our bodies created— starting at four months into the womb—were its best guess at how to survive. Our bodies picked one from a pool of 30,000 different responses available. Catapult 20 years later and we are no longer likely in the same environment (though we often create environments that support our patterns). We might find ourselves saying things like, "I never," "I always" and perhaps this is the one piece that keeps getting in the way of our happiness. In fact, when a person lands in my office it is often a painful, confusing, distressing, life altering; "I'm tired of this happening over and over again" kind of angst. This is the motivation and the opportunity for my clients (and you!) to make a change.

What I like about this science is that other established approaches and theories dovetail nicely with it such as the developmental attachment formation stages, the functional phases of expressive arts therapy, cognitive behavioral therapy, metaphysics, neurobiology, quantum theory and IQM. Throw in thoughts about learning styles, levels of awareness and their kinetic calibration, merge with client's unique experiences and responses and now we're vibrating change.

INTENTIONAL LIVING

These three areas culminate into my philosophy of intentional living: A healthy balance of spiritual intelligence, physical, mental and emotional health, trusting relationships, and meaningful work. Which puts us straight back in the driver's seat with the understanding that we alone are responsible for the world we create. The question at its core is; "If you create your world, why wouldn't you want one in which you were happy?"

My fairy godmother knew I would find my happiness and I think she was onto the simplicity of the matter when she said "You don't ask for much..." For it really is quite simple, we need only shift our gaze. The question is, *how* do we shift our gaze? Often we need the assistance of a guide and more information. When we break down the patterns of our lives, they become more tangible, they transform into opportunities and teach us how to discern between our bodies and Ourselves. Which in the end leads us closer to our truth and our true purpose on this earth.....to evolve.

CHAPTER 2:

ARE YOU PREPARED?

YOU ARE ON A JOURNEY OF POTENTIALLY INTENSE WORK. Once you start you can't unknow what you learn. It is also a time to allow yourself to know what you already know. You might have times where you think to yourself: "Well, of course! I should have known this!" You might have times where you feel uncomfortable, and your inclination will be to stop because of this uncomfortable feeling. It's important for you to know a couple things.

Layout of this Guidebook: Each chapter begins with a story from my life. Woven together are moments, events, reflections, and clarity learned over time. Each chapter has a purpose and an area of growth that ends with an experiment that allows you to build skills, reflect on your life and find clarity. Each chapter builds on the next, providing guidance along the way. You will want to complete the experiments in each chapter before going on to the next chapter.

Pacing of this workbook: Take your time and go at the pace that feels comfortable to you. You should feel *just* uncomfortable enough to understand that you are growing and challenging old norms. Nobody likes to feel "bad" and your body doesn't either. As a result, our bodies have acquired behaviors to defend against the "bad" feeling. Part of your process will be in seeing your defenses as coping strategies that your body has acquired to help you feel better and to avoid pain and discomfort. Emotional pain is no different from a cut or sprain to our physical body. We would not ignore the cut or sprain. We would attend to it and help ease the pain. And we would know that it would heal eventually. We would even get help if the cut was too deep for us to manage on our own or if that sprain didn't heal within a few days. So, like emotional pain, we do what we can on our own and when it persists, we need to seek help to manage it further.

Acknowledge what you know: Likely, you have found strategies to manage your emotional pain that have helped you feel better. In this chapter, I want you to take the time to acknowledge these skills and strategies as well as possibly suggest other strategies that you will want to have before you begin your journey. We'll begin by looking at where you are right now. The exercises in this chapter will guide you to assess what you know and will point to where you will want to grow.

DATA COLLECTING—RESEARCH #1

Energy Input and Energy Output

Listed below are several areas that make up the entirety of what it means to be human. In each category is a scale under specific questions that reflect activities that you might engage. The goal here is to take a pause and really think about how much energy you are putting into each area.

As you look through these questions, attempt to be as honest with yourself as possible. There are no right or wrong answers, only your own reflections on how you live day to day. You might find that you have judgments and opinions and feel that these questions are prompting you to make changes. You may find that you "know" that you are doing the right thing for you or not and I would encourage you to tune into that "knowing" voice. You are unique in how you respond to your life and this exercise is to help you become more aware of your uniqueness.

PHYSICAL

Never   1   2   -3   4   5   Always
I don't drink caffeine

Never   1   2   -3   4   5   Always
I drink water throughout the day

Never   1   2   -3   4   5   Always
I keep my body groomed and clean

Never   1   2   -3   4   5   Always
I don't drink alcohol

Never   1   2   -3   4   5   Always
I don't smoke

Never   1   2   -3   4   5   Always
I exercise regularly

Never   1   2   -3   4   5   Always
I stretch my body

Never   1   2   -3   4   5   Always
I sleep at least eight hours each night

Never   1   2   -3   4   5   Always
I eat well balanced meals every day

Never   1   2   -3   4   5   Always
I have safe housing

Never   1   2   -3   4   5   Always
I don't have any physical pain or issues

Never   1   2   -3   4   5   Always
I am comfortable with my sexual life

What stands out for you?

_____

_____

In what area(s) do you focus your energy? (a 3, 4 or 5)

_____

_____

In what area(s) do you withhold your energy? (a 1 or 2)

_____

_____

EMOTIONAL

Never   1   2   -3   4   5   Always
I feel a variety of feelings including sadness, joy, anger

Never   1   2   -3   4   5   Always
I feel a variety of feelings including sadness, joy, anger

Never   1   2   -3   4   5   Always
I have the ability to control my emotions

Never   1   2   -3   4   5   Always
I easily express my emotions to others

Never   1   2   -3   4   5   Always
I have a group of friends who meet my needs

Never   1   2   -3   4   5   Always
I have a best friend

Never   1   2   -3   4   5   Always
My friends and family accept me for who I am

Never   1   2   -3   4   5   Always
Everything in my home environment is just how I want it

Never   1   2   -3   4   5   Always

Everything in my work environment is just how I want it

Never   1   2   -3   4   5   Always

I hug someone every day

Never   1   2   -3   4   5   Always

I don't have any unspoken words between me and my immediate family

Never   1   2   -3   4   5   Always

I say "no" when it is in my best interest

Never   2   3   3   4   5   Always

I feel good about how I manage money

What stands out for you?

_____

_____

In what area(s) do you focus your energy? (a 3, 4 or 5)

_____

_____

In what area(s) do you withhold your energy? (1 or 2)

_____

_____

MENTAL/INTELLECTUAL. PSYCHOLOGICAL

Never   1   2   -3   4   5   Always
I am aware of my thoughts most of the time

Never   1   2   -3   4   5   Always
My thoughts about myself reflect my fundamental goodness

Never   1   2   -3   4   5   Always
I am able to redirect my thoughts

Never   1   2   -3   4   5   Always
I can quiet my mind when I want to

Never   1   2   -3   4   5   Always
At times I will receive spontaneous flashes of insight in my mind

Never   1   2   -3   4   5   Always
I can self-reflect

Never   1   2   -3   4   5   Always
I keep a journal where I write out my thoughts and feelings

Never   1   2   -3   4   5   Always
I have a hobby

Never   1   2   -3   4   5   Always
I ask and receive help

Never   1   2   -3   4   5   Always
I read for pleasure

Never   1   2   -3   4   5   Always
I regularly take the time to learn something new outside of
my work

Never   1   2   -3   4   5   Always
I regularly engage in some kind of professional
development

Never   1   2   -3   4   5   Always
I turn off small electronics at some point during the day for
several hours

Never   1   2   -3   4   5   Always
I feel confident and self-assured

Never   1   2   -3   4   5   Always
I interact easily with others

Never   1   2   -3   4   5   Always
I know that I have power over my circumstances

Never   1   2   -3   4   5   Always
I listen to others and feel heard

What stands out for you?

_____

_____

In what area(s) do you focus your energy? (a 3, 4 or 5)

_____

_____

In what area(s) do you withhold your energy? (a 1 or 2)

_____

_____

SPIRITUAL

Never   1   2   -3   4   5   Always
I go into nature regularly

Never   1   2   -3   4   5   Always
I have reflected on what "spiritual" means to me

Never   1   2   -3   4   5   Always
I set aside time each day to meditate or contemplate

Never   1   2   -3   4   5   Always
I am often grateful

Never   1   2   -3   4   5   Always
I listen to music I love every day

Never   1   2   -3   4   5   Always

I notice and appreciate something about nature every day

Never   1   2   -3   4   5   Always

I know my life has meaning and purpose and can articulate my core values

Never   1   2   -3   4   5   Always

My work is important to me

Never   1   2   -3   4   5   Always

I regularly receive spiritual guidance

Never   1   2   -3   4   5   Always

I imagine and manifest my visions easily

Never   1   2   -3   4   5   Always

I know what is going to happen or be said before it does

Never   1   2   -3   4   5   Always

I am frequently inspired

Never   1   2   -3   4   5   Always

I view the world as a learning experience for my growth

Never   1   2   -3   4   5   Always

I breathe deeply and mindfully

What stands out for you?

_____

_____

In what area(s) do you focus your energy? (a 3, 4 or 5)

_____

_____

In what area(s) do you withhold your energy? (a 1 or 2)

_____

_____

Now that you have an idea where you focus and give yourself energy and withhold or deplete yourself of energy, do not fall into the trap of learning this new information about your life to state that you are a failure (or a success). You can't change something you don't know anything about, and you can't celebrate and appreciate all that you do if you don't acknowledge it!

DATA COLLECTING—RESEARCH #2

STAGES OF CHANGE

You are constantly in the process of change in lots of different areas of your life. People have identified this for a very long time. For example, the I Ching is a book about identifying what stage of change you are in. Rather than go into the ancient rites and rituals of Chinese culture we can look at the more-Western concepts. The process of picking out this book to read was one part of your life that is now already in a stage of change. The stages of change detailed below delineate the process that all humans go through. As you look through the different stages, know that this is like a dance that we move in and out of. If you feel stuck , simply use this information to remind yourself that you are not failing, you are in a stage of change. You can be in several different stages of change at one time with several different areas of your life. Revisit these stages as you make your way through this guidebook and the lessons identified for each chapter, then identify which stage you are in with each concept addressed.

PRECONTEMPLATION. CONTEMPLATION. DETERMINATION. ACTION. MAINTENANCE. TERMINATION

FIRST STAGE—PRECONTEMPLATION:

If you are in this stage of making changes, you are not even thinking about making a change. You don't see a problem that you need to change even if you are getting feedback from others, you will dismiss it as valid. If you are in this stage but being told to make a change, consider if you are one of these types of precontemplators:

- **Reluctant**—You don't want to change, and the impact of the problem has not fully surfaced.
- **Rebellious**—You may have a big investment in what you are currently doing and don't like being told what to do.
- **Resigned**—You have given up hope that you could even make a change and are overwhelmed by the problem.

- **Rationalizing**—You have all the answers as to why there is no problem to change and that change just isn't for you.

Are you in this stage of change in any area of your life?

_____

_____

    To move through this stage you might need to get honest with yourself, take time to listen to what you tell yourself and as you work through this book and become more aware of your inner voice, be open to the messages that you hear.

Notes:

_____

_____

_____

_____

_____

_____

_____

_____

Second Stage—Contemplation:

If you are in this stage of making changes you are now willing to consider the idea that there is something to change but you might be neutral about it or undecided. You are considering the pros and cons and the barriers to making the change. You might be thinking about previous attempts you have made and what didn't work in the past.

Are you in this stage of change in any area of your life?

_____

_____

_____

To move through this stage, imagine what you might do to begin, think about what you would do if you were to make a change, visualize yourself making a change and what support or information you might need in order to feel prepared. Write out a pros and cons list and what you want to accomplish and why.

Notes:

_____

_____

_____

_____

THIRD STAGE—PREPARATION:

At this stage, you have decided to make a change and are preparing to do it. You have weighed all the pros and cons, you understand what's at risk and the rewards involved and this has tipped you into preparing. You are ready and committed to action.

Are you in this stage of change in any area of your life?

_____

_____

_____

To move through this stage you might do things like research, getting equipment, or hiring a coach or mentor. Or maybe this is why you are reading this book! You can pick a start date, plan out a structure, tell friends or family about the change you want to make, in general build the excitement and your confidence.

Notes:

_____

_____

_____

_____

FOURTH STAGE—ACTION:

You are doing it, something new! It is in this stage that you learn about what is working and what is not working and the dance may begin back into precontemplation or preparing to look at a different approach. You also might still revert back to "old" habits and ways in this stage and have to try and keep regrouping with the new behavior. The important part of this stage is that you are making efforts to make a change at times.

Are you in this stage of change in any area of your life?

_____

_____

To move through this stage, admit what is working and what isn't working and make modifications. Notice when making the change is more difficult and keep making the choice of the new behavior and why you are doing it.

Notes:

_____

_____

_____

_____

_____

FIFTH STAGE—MAINTENANCE:

You are finding that you are stepping into the change that you wanted more than not. There is a magic formula here of around six months of repetition with your new behavior. This means that your efforts are taking hold long enough to feel confident that you *can* make and *did* make a change. Celebrate your accomplishment and acknowledge all that went into making it happen. Remind yourself of the reasons for the change and look for the results you wanted. Notice what is working for you and keep those structures or supports active. Notice when you don't have these structures or support that it might be harder. You may notice that you are treating challenges in a new way, as a way of learning something more about yourself.

Are you in this stage of change in any area of your life?

_____

_____

Notes:

_____

_____

_____

_____

LAST STAGE OF CHANGE—TERMINATION:

You have now been making your change for more than six months. You may be looking back and wondering how you could ever have done anything differently in the past. At this stage of change you have fully adopted the new behavior you wanted and gained what you set out to do. Your new behavior is now a part of your lifestyle and you can't imagine doing anything differently. You also might have discovered more changes that you would like to make and you are much more confident as you begin your next goal.

Are you in this stage of change in any area of your life?

_____

_____

Notes:

_____

_____

_____

_____

_____

_____

DATA COLLECTING—RESEARCH #3

LEARNING STYLES

Another consideration when we want to make a change is our learning style. We all learn in different ways, and they fall into three categories. As you look at the information below, determine whether you are predominately a visual, auditory, or kinesthetic/tactile learner. Understand you may be a combination of all three, and that's okay. In the end, the best learning happens when we combine them. If you are lacking in one area this might be a place to grow your skill.

Notice the learning style that is easiest for you and as you go through this book know that you will use this learning style to learn what is being presented to you. For example, if I suggest imagining something but you are a kinesthetic learner you might write out the instructions or take a walk in order to think more clearly about what I have suggested. Start with your strength, then challenge yourself throughout this book to build the muscle of using one or two of the other learning styles that don't come as easy for you.

IF YOU ARE A VISUAL LEARNER:

When you ...

Spell	Do you try to see the word?
Talk	Would you rather talk than listen? Do you often use words like see, picture, and imagine?
Concentrate	Do you get distracted by your environment?
Meet someone	Do you remember their face before you remember their name?
Read	Do you like descriptive scenes and picture what you are reading?
Do something new	Do you like to see demonstrations, slides and posters?
Put something together	Do you look at the directions and the pictures?

Notes:

_____

_____

_____

_____

IF YOU ARE AN AUDITORY LEARNER

When you...

Spell	Do you sound out the word?
Talk	Do you enjoy listening? Do you often use words like hear, tune in and think?
Concentrate	Are you distracted by sounds and noises?
Meet someone	Do you forget their face but remember their name or what you talked about?
Read	Do you enjoy the dialogue and conversation of the characters?
Do something new	Do you prefer verbal instructions or someone talking about it?
Put something together	Do you call the help desk or ask someone else for help?

NOTES:

_____

_____

_____

_____

IF YOU ARE A KINESTHETIC & TACTILE LEARNER

When you...

Spell	Do you write the word?
Talk	Do you gesture frequently and often use words like feel, touch, and hold?
Concentrate	Are you distracted by activity around you?
Meet someone	Do you remember what you did together?
Read	Do you prefer not to read or if you do read, do you like action stories?
Do something new	Do you jump right in?
Put something together	Do you ignore the directions and figure it out as you go?

NOTES:

_____

_____

_____

_____

JOURNAL, SPACE, AND TIME

Before you begin you will want to have a notebook or journal to write in as a companion to this book which provides spaces for your thoughts as you go along. You will also want to consider the best time of day to read this book, as well as a safe, comforting place to be with yourself as you work through the exercises.

SET YOUR INTENTION:

What would you like to focus on throughout this guidebook?

_____

_____

What would you like to learn?

_____

_____

How would you like to grow?

_____

_____

How will you know you have achieved success?

_____

_____

What are questions you want answered?

_____

_____

Other Intentions:

_____

_____

_____

_____

_____

_____

_____

MOVING ON

You are ready to move on to the next chapter when you have completed all the research and gathered your data as well as set your intentions.

CHAPTER THREE:

ONE DEEP BREATH

I N THIS CHAPTER YOU WILL TAKE THE FIRST STEPS AT BECOMING aware, slowing down so that you can really listen to your thoughts and to your feelings.

I have struggled with anxiety all my life but I didn't even realize it. When I think back, I realize and now understand the reasons for my stomach pain, trouble sleeping, extreme shyness in social situations, lack of confidence, fear, increased need to organize and control situations and people, to plan ahead, and times when I got into a "stubborn" loop when things didn't go "the right way" (really just my imagined way). Do you recognize yourself here? I do hear variations of these same sentiments from my clients regularly.

One day in Phoenix I was driving from one meeting to the next. Even today, I remember the stretch of freeway I was on. It was another sunny day in Arizona, the light reflecting off the other cars around me, the concrete desert laid out with lines guiding us all to our destinations. This stretch of road is a tricky one, everyone is going at least 65 mph, there are eight lanes and three highways merging to one with my upcoming exit six lanes to the right in less than a quarter of a mile. If that wasn't stressful enough, I was late. Not only was I driving, I was also thinking of the recent and not-so-recent past, of the immediate future and even farther into the future. I was on autopilot when it came to my present situation. My past thoughts consisted of flashes of the previous weekend at my expressive arts intensive workshop, my recent separation and impending divorce, my mom and dad, and all the emotions that came with those thoughts –expectation, sadness, anger, grief, loss. My future thoughts were bound up in the meeting I was about to be late for, wondering if the kids were getting to aftercare, how I'd be picking them up later, what's in the house for dinner, how much homework will they have, will there be time for a bath, the chores that need to be done, will sleep come tonight? And the most intense future thought, "I AM GOING TO BE LATE."

I snap back to the present moment, the one where I'm on autopilot driving. "I need to get over," I realized, and at that moment, everything else fell away. As I get into my lane and am safely exiting onto the next highway—oh and by the way, this is not an exit where you slow down to stop, this stretch of highway quickly puts you into your next trajectory at the same high speed along with the other six cars speeding around you. I look at the clock on my dashboard and see that it is 10 minutes until the meeting starts. I visualize the entire route to my destination, and it hits me: " I'M NOT LATE YET." "I'm not late yet! "I am not late yet, the meeting doesn't start for 10 minutes, and I am not late yet. I'm here, right now, safely in the right lane, in my car, in sunny Arizona, and I'm not late yet." In this present moment I am not late. I took a deep breath and for the next 10 minutes in which I was not late, I relaxed, I reassured myself, I enjoyed the rest of the ride, time stopped, somehow I became fully present. I took deep breaths, reassured myself, brought myself to the present, and realized that when I did, my mind stopped thinking of all those past and future thoughts.

Today it is a common practice, and everyone seems to know that you are to take deep breaths when you are anxious, but honestly, I didn't understand this. My first puzzle piece to this revelation didn't come until I took Lamaze classes with my first pregnancy. It was here that I learned how to breathe, deep belly breaths, in through the nose and out through the mouth at an equal pace. Later when I took yoga classes and learned meditation, I learned variations on this theme and how purposeful breathing could be applied even outside of pregnancy!

So even remembering to take a deep breath at that moment on the freeway is something I had to learn in various ways at various points in my life. I realized that smoking a cigarette back in the day was my way of taking a deep breath. In anxious moments, I would think, "I need to smoke a cigarette" instead of "I need to take a deep breath." I also was a big runner in high school and all the way into my late 40s. I didn't know it at the time but by running I relieved all the anxious energy I was carrying around and also relieved stress. Running forced those deep breaths into my lungs and moving my muscles forced all that energy through my veins and out my feet. It would slow down my mind's chatter and I felt in control, powerful. When I was a child I would ride my bike all around town and I loved to swim, immersing myself into the water where it was quiet. On the high school swim team I would do laps to the point I was sweating in the water—working my lungs. These were all the coping strategies I had up until that point but didn't even know I had them, until I was not using them as often. As an adult I had put the regularity of running, biking and swimming aside to raise children, and make a living to raise children. Slowly the anxiety had built back up in my body, as I continued the same old pattern of overthinking, worrying, planning and striving toward perfection in the eyes of others' expectations of me, which of course I had taken on for my own.

Later, when I studied the biology of the brain, I would learn that the brain is just another body part, just like my hand is a body part. I was elated by this perspective. My hand is meant for small motor skills, and I have taught it to write, and I can use it when I want to write and I can stop writing whenever I want. The brain is meant for thinking, but it can only think in the past or the future. When the brain thinks in the past it pulls from memory. The fond memories of a good time, or a person, place or thing. Once when I was robbed of all of my jewelry I drew out every single piece as I remembered it so that I would not forget it. The mind can learn from these memories, it makes assumptions and patterns about them so that we don't make mistakes again and we can feel mastery over things as a consequence.

It can invoke the same emotions from the past as we remember. The brain might conjure up thoughts that then lead us to feel regret, loss, shame, guilt, disappointment, grief, apathy, anger or hopelessness. When we have too many of these types of thoughts or experiences we can feel low energy, and we are actually vibrating a slow, draining energy. When we have too many of these types of thoughts and emotions our energy is pulled down and we may feel depressed.

The brain can also think into the future and this activity has its good qualities just like learning from our past does. As we think into the future we can plan, solve, prevent disaster, look forward to upcoming events. And, when we feel we have prepared for our safety, feel in control, and apply learned skills, we can feel hopefulness, pride and courage. If we think too far into the future we can get anxious, fearful, and trapped in past patterns. But when we take one deep breath, in that nano of a second our brain does not think of the past or the future. Try it! You might have to link several breaths together to actually notice this, but the brain will stop thinking during that deep breath. It's amazing! You don't have to sit yogi style in a monastery, in silence, from dawn to dusk, without cares, worries, or distractions to feel the immediate effects of stopping the mind. And we all have time to take ONE DEEP BREATH, no matter where we are, no matter what we are doing. We are already breathing anyway, let's just make it productive. Our body recognizes that we must breathe to continue living. It learned this mere moments after we were born, when the flap closed in the heart chamber that was getting oxygen from the mother.

Practice this deep intentional breath by placing your hand on your chest. As you inhale feel your lungs expand. As you exhale feel your belly rise and soften. You might even notice a baby breathing and see that this is how they do it. We learn later to control our breath, in various increments and some, once they began to focus on the breath, realized that they were often literally holding their breath. In case you are concerned about how you look to others, taking a deep breath can be done without anyone really noticing. And I look forward to the day when you no longer are focusing outside of yourself and adapting.

Once you slow down your thoughts you can direct it's thinking to what you want to think, and you can direct your brain to stop thinking—with one deep breath or five for a dramatic effect. If you take one deep breath every hour in addition to times you are having any kind of feeling, then you will have begun training your brain. Your thoughts will slow down as a result. This is an important step because part of living an intentional life is to catch your thoughts, and you can't catch something that is going too fast.

We are often taught to not focus too much on our thoughts. We minimize, dismiss them, say to ourselves, "I don't want to think about it. " I remember my mom calling it "navel gazing" and she would say it with judgement, implying that it was a waste of time.

I can see her perspective. She grew up on a farm in the depression, her family having immigrated from Germany. On the family farm, she was part of a team that had to work 24/7. There was no time to think or indulge in any thoughts or feelings that were contrary to this survival. As a consequence, there is a high rate of farmers who are depressed and/or commit suicide. Clearly that approach isn't working. If you want to read more, here is one article on the subject of depression and suicide in farmers across the globe (https://www.ncbi.nlm.nih.gov/pmc/articles/PMC2802368/). Nonetheless, talking about our thoughts and emotions was not a part of my family experience. When my older brother was in high school he was at risk for failing and started getting into legal trouble. As a family we began attending family therapy sessions at Menninger's Foundation. I dreaded these sessions. At the time I had enough to deal with already. I had just started junior high in a new school where I only had two friends from Girl Scouts. I would ride my bike to and from school every day except when we had our family sessions. In these sessions, I would sit with my head down, avoiding eye contact and anything remotely connected to speaking. I would not have known what to say anyway. I didn't understand why we were there and especially why *I* was there. I do remember vividly the man and woman who facilitated these sessions. This was in the 70s and women wore pantyhose and heels as part of business attire. As I sat quietly with my head bent down I noticed that the woman therapist had the longest leg hair underneath her hose that I'd ever seen. I also remember my mom doing a lot of controlled yelling, lots of hard energy flying around that room and what seemed like no solutions or resolutions or good feelings ever. One night at home when the fighting between my brother and my mom got so loud, it woke me up from a deep sleep. I gathered all my courage ,my pillow and quickly and quietly went down two flights of stairs to our basement, where I hoped it would be quieter. No one asked me what I was feeling, no one came to talk with me about anything that was happening upstairs. Even if they had I would not likely have been able to tell them.

My "normal" was being invisible, unseen, unheard and I got comfortable there. I didn't know what I was thinking anyway, I was all the feels. But I did draw and play the piano, guitar, ukulele, recorder and I sang. I poured myself into making art and remember drawing with charcoal one day after school. The drawing was a window in my bedroom and without thinking I drew a crack in that window, I shaded it in and felt the brokenness of it and felt complete. It wasn't good or bad in my mind, it was my truth. My mom happened to walk in about that time and tears came to her eyes as she said: "Life seems to be like that." I used drawing to express myself when my voice had no words. When I drew, I was also intensely focused on the drawing. A single, intentional focus, and while I didn't realize it at the time, my mind was free from its chatter. I felt peace and calm when I drew. I was creating something outside of myself and I energetically took what was inside of me and put it in a place that no longer created uncomfortableness in my body. This also worked when I would play the piano or guitar and sing along. A single focus, concentration and mostly beautiful music, moving the energy out of my body. In college, there was a rare moment when I was alone from my three other roommates, and I poured my heart and soul out into my guitar and singing. I got a call from the dorm room upstairs telling me to turn down the music on my radio. I couldn't get away from the world telling me to silence myself. Later, when I studied expressive arts therapy I was free from the perfection that society places on the creative arts and reclaimed freedom and expression as the first expectation. Just like the cracked window in my drawing, art isn't always pretty or comfortable, especially if it is reflecting uncomfortable feelings.

If you are one of those people that doesn't understand why you feel the way you do, or if you can't even identify what you are feeling, you likely have a lot of thoughts that are going unnoticed. The thing is that we have very few original thoughts. We are thinking the same thing over and over and we're feeling the same thing over and over. It's time to get off the endless loop of the freeway in our head, take the next exit and relax, slow your thoughts down so you can catch them, and identify the emotions they are creating.

As I drove on that freeway that sunny day in Arizona, I took a deep breath, I caught my thoughts, I realized that I was feeling anxious, and instead of driving unaware, I checked the behavior of my mind and came fully into the present. In that moment I challenged my automatic response of my amygdala, the part of the brain that processes fear and threats and created a new pattern of response.

I rewired my brain.

"I'm not late yet."

I stopped my anxiety response. It's important to note that I could only do this in an anxiety-provoking state. My amygdala had to be engaged in its automatic stress response to learn that it was creating my stress!

SUMMARY:

Learning to slow down helps with thought-invoking anxiety. Slowing down helps you to hear and actively listen to your thoughts and feelings. Awareness of your thoughts and feelings is necessary to understand how you operate in your world. Imagine that you are a worker in a chocolate factory and you are responsible for putting the finishing dollop on the top of each chocolate piece going along on a conveyer belt. If the conveyer belt is going too fast you won't be able to attend to each chocolate. Just like your thoughts and feelings, if they are coming too fast you don't really manage them, soon they build up and you become overwhelmed. The experiments below are designed for you to learn the skill of slowing down your thoughts, calming your body, so you can tune into your thoughts and feelings. This is a skill that will compound over time, and you will continue to use them throughout the guidebook. You will likely feel a shift within a week of doing the three experiments below.

EXPERIMENT #1

BREATHE AND FIND THE GAP BETWEEN THOUGHTS

From six months in the womb to four-years old we have been creating patterns to our environment. Our body will pick one from 30,000 different options to survive in this world. Our bodies are survival machines, and we learned these patterns of responses really well, even before we were consciously aware. We learned from others, our environments and in turn our body made the DNA, the genes and the chemical responses needed to build a pattern of response.

Our brains then made categories of association, and it learned fast and well "if this happens, I do this." During this first stage of life training, we slept a lot and so we were in a *theta* state of mind, which is also the exact wave that the brain goes into when we meditate or conduct even the smallest meditation—a deep breath. The conscious mind steps aside and the subconscious, with its imagery and patternmaking, steps in. To inhibit this automatic response will take awareness. This is where the deep breath comes in.

When you take a deep breath you will stop thinking.

When you stop thinking you can then become the observer of your thoughts and your emotions. In this experiment you will begin to take deep breaths, every hour and as often as you remember, and you will take deep breaths when you are having an emotion.

Set an alarm on your phone or your watch to go off every hour to remind you to take a deep breath. Like Pavlov's dogs, you will begin to automatically respond. Consider transition times in your day as opportunities to take a deep breath. When you finish one task and go on to another, take a deep breath, when you get in your car, take a deep breath, waiting in line, take a deep breath, at a stop light, take a deep breath. You may forget at first, but this step of your transformation is critical to your overall mastery over your life.

Some people who begin this experiment realize that they have been holding their breath. If you do too, take a deep breath.

Notes:

_____

_____

_____

_____

_____

_____

_____

EXPERIMENT #2

NOTICE WHAT YOU'RE THINKING

When you take a deep breath, think about what your brain was just thinking. I want to be able to walk up to you at any given moment of the day and ask you: "What are you thinking?" and you will be able to tell me your thoughts.

Catch your thoughts. Every time you take a deep breath, check in to see what you were thinking. Write down your findings. Look for patterns of thoughts, and themes that may emerge. When I first started capturing my thoughts I realized that most of them were critical, judging types of messages. Later I realized these weren't my thoughts at all but my perception of the world I received in my early years from other people and experiences and had taken up for my own. Because I slowed them down, I learned I had a choice, I could receive these thoughts or reject them. I was in control of the body part known as my mind.

Next, label your thoughts. Imagine that you stick these labels on file folders. For each thought put them in the appropriate folder, then close the file.

This is a past thought,

This is a future thought,

This isn't my thought,

I've thought of this before,

I don't need to think about this right now,

And any other labels you can think of.....

Notes:

_____

_____

_____

_____

_____

_____

_____

_____

EXPERIMENT #3

IDENTIFY THE EMOTION YOU ARE FEELING

When you take a deep breath, think about what you are feeling. Name the emotion(s) and think back to what you were thinking. I want to be able to walk up to you at any given moment of the day and ask you: "What are you feeling?" and you will be able to tell me what you are feeling.

While in the throes of emotion, we sometimes can identify the biggest one we are feeling. In this experiment you may find that once you identify the obvious emotion, there are perhaps additional emotions as well. For example, when that reckless driver in their bright red car sped past us on the freeway we got angry, but we also felt scared and surprised. The next time you catch yourself "acting out your emotions," **stop**. Right there in the middle of your actions, take a deep breath, ask yourself: "What am I feeling, and what am I thinking?" You can actually have an emotion without acting it out. Instead name the emotion, by naming it we have acknowledge that we are experiencing an emotion and we have identified it. Once labeled we can decide if we want to further examine it—we can understand the meaning we have attached to it. Do we want this feeling? Does it reflect our beliefs? Does this emotion hold the whole truth of our experience? When you tune into your emotions, you might use the list of emotional words below to identify and name them.

When you are having an emotion—take a deep breath, become the observer of your body and ask your body: "What emotion am I feeling?"

Notes:

_____

_____

_____

_____

_____

_____

EMOTION WORDS

Absorbed	Adventurous	Affectionate	Afraid
Alarmed	Annoyed	Angry	Anxious
Alert	Alive	Amazed	Amused
Animated	Appreciated	Ardent	Aroused
Astonished	Bewildered	Bitter	Bored
Blissful	Breathless	Buoyant	Calm
Carefree	Cheerful	Cold	Concerned

Confused	Cross	Comfortable	Complacent
Composed	Concerned	Confident	content
Cool	Curious	Dazzled	Dejected
Depressed	Detached	Disappointed	Discouraged
Distressed	Delighted	Eager	Ecstatic
Edgy	Embarrassed	Exasperated	Elated
Enchanted	Encouraged	Excited	Expansive
Expectant	Fascinated	Fatigued	Fearful
Forlorn	Furious	Free	Friendly
Glad	Gleeful	Glowing	Good-humored
Grateful	Guilty	Gloomy	Happy
heavy	Helpful	Hostile	Hurt
Hopeful	Impatient	Indifferent	Intense
Irritated	Inquisitive	Inspired	Irate
Interested	Inspired	Intense	Intrigued
Invigorated	Involved	Jealous	Joyful
Jubilant	Keyed -up	Lazy	Listless
Lonely	Loving	Mad	Mean
Miserable	Mournful	Mellow	Merry
Mindful	Moved	Nervous	Numb
Optimistic	Overwhelmed	Peaceful	Perplexed
Panicky	Pessimistic	Puzzled	Pleasant
Pleased	Proud	Quiet	Refreshed

Reluctant	Resentful	Restless	Relaxed
Relieved	Sad	scared	Satisfied
Sorrowful	Spiritless	suspicious	Shaky
Shocked	Secure	Sensitive	Serene
Stimulated	Surprised	Tender	Tepid
Terrified	Tired	Troubled	Thankful
Thrilled	Touched	Trusting	Upbeat
Uncomfortable	Uneasy	Upset	Uptight
Vexed	Warm	Weary	Withdrawn
Worried	Wonderful	Zestful	Zoned-out

MOVING ON

Move on to the next chapter after you have completed these three experiments for a week. Continue to use these skills as you go through the guidebook and your skill will continue to grow. You will continue to feel a shift in your day to day experiences.

CHAPTER FOUR:

BODY AWARENESS

WE LIVE IN A HUMAN BODY, AND JUST LIKE WHEN WE drive in a car it is necessary to understand its working parts, know when it is running correctly, know how to ensure it can run correctly and know when to fix it. Our bodies, like our cars, will not run if we don't do some basic things to maintain them. Gas, oil, fluids, belts... we can choose to keep our car clean and welcoming for others to sit in or not. We can choose the way we drive as well. I often wonder if the way that people drive their car is how they approach their world as well. The driver who is tentative to merge, or change lanes, are they likely to also be tentative in life, struggling to ask for what they want or need, or afraid to offend others or go out of their way to please others? The person who flashes their lights behind you to tell you to get over or yells or glares at you when they pass, are they also looking at their world as in their way. Do they blame others for their "bad luck?' Do they avoid taking responsibility for their words and actions and how they affect others? Or the careless driver, whether by distraction, thoughtlessness or lack of planning, or doing too many things at one time, do they float from day to day in a fog, unaware, distracted by anything that catches their attention, lucky to make it safely to any destination or achieve what they want?

We take our bodies for granted—maybe like we do our cars. We just expect them to run and when they don't we are inconvenienced.

We can be much more proactive with our cars and our bodies and everything else. Maybe you have come to realize that what you have been putting into your body is negative, and energy-draining instead of "high quality gasoline."

Maybe you have come to realize that you have not been maintaining your body well enough to keep it in working order. Maybe you realize that you have not been focused on your destination enough to get there. If you use a GPS to get to your destination, is it taking you where you want to go? Have you given it the right information? When we take a turn that isn't recommended by the GPS, it will begin by telling you to make turns to get you back to the original route. If you go too far off of that route or ignore it long enough, it will finally accept the new starting point and state "re-routing." Like the GPS, you can do this with the neurotransmitters of your brain. You are in charge of how and where you are going, and the body will re-route. Just like the GPS, it will fight you for a bit, then accept the new starting point and re-route. At that moment in your body, you have made a new pathway in your neurons. Your body, like your car, doesn't care where it goes and how it gets there, it just wants to drive, and in the case of your body—it wants to survive.

Have you ever been driving along and thought, "I think it's time for an oil change" or "those tires should be checked." If you listened to that small voice and acted on it ,you likely avoided the consequence of not having the maintenance on your car. Well, our bodies are the same, they are giving you indicators all the time of what you need to do. We often ignore them, but not always. We'll stretch out a stiff muscle, we'll drink some water when we are thirsty. But a lot of us are on autopilot, allowing our body's GPS to drive us around while taking our route for granted. We will ignore that pain in the neck until it really hurts and we seek massage therapy, chiropractors and medication. We'll plow ahead and lift that heavy desk onto the truck and pay for it later. Or we'll ignore those negative thoughts and feel depressed and wonder why. Or let our minds run crazy with worry and fears and all the future tasks and to-dos until we are in a sweat with panic. We'll dismiss these things by saying, "it's my depression or anxiety again "without thinking through how we got there and how we could have prevented it.

When we are young our body, like a new car, runs pretty well without much attention. But just like an old car, as we get older all that wear, tear and abuse we gave our new body/car starts to catch up with it. Either young or old, our bodies are sending us messages all the time. And we can check in with it, tune in to it and feel the sensations. When we don't check in with it often it will only amp up its messages, like the check engine lights on your dashboard. We'll get used to that pain in the back, neck, knee, and we accept it.

But would we accept this kind of functioning from our cars?

Maybe, but would that keep the car around as long as possible. The problem is this is our only body, we can get a new car, in theory, whenever we want. Or even get around by other means. Our body is the only way we get around.

So I guess I'm trying to convince you to take care of your body, to know how it works for you. And to see how you have adapted your world to fit how it is functioning.

Around Christmas time one year I decided to buy my older kids an Xbox and hopped online to find the best price (red flag #1). I found it and what a deal! It required that I send a money order (red flag #2), which I had never done but what a price and I really wanted to surprise my kids and have them admire me for my progressiveness and for being so in tune with meeting their greatest desires (red flag #3). I went to the closest grocery store and figured out how to send off money to this website. As I walked out of the grocery store the automatic doors opening with a whoosh of air blasting on me, at that same moment I felt a punch in my stomach like I had just gotten the wind knocked out of me. I doubled over and stifled a whoof so that people passing by wouldn't think I was losing it. It literally hit me, I realized I had made a big, perhaps expensive mistake. I had ignored all the small red flags going up in my head and now they amped up to a punch in my stomach. Now in a panic, I rushed to my car and back to my computer to find that the website had been shut down. Fraud! I called the grocery store and they said that the money order had not gone through, and I canceled it.

I grew up with stomach aches and lower back pain, these sensations were my normal, I always felt these aches and pains. I didn't realize how much I was feeling from others around me. I took these feelings in as my own and kept them there without knowledge of what to do with them let alone identify or name them. So, my body took over, and managed them. "Oh" it would say, "you're feeling anxious, let me give you a stomachache since you're not understanding it." Or a backache when I wasn't feeling emotionally supported. Often our bodies will provide a handy metaphor for us. The dog pulls the leash without listening to your direction to heel and I think, "man, he's a pain in the neck" and I get a pain in my neck from the yank on the leash. If I understand the frustration, listen to my thoughts and emotions I can learn from this event. Then I pull out my dog-training skills, slow down or be more patient. And I avoid actually getting a pain in my neck from repeated yanks from my dog on his leash.

Of course, sometimes we can make a clear connection to our pain. I fell down the stairs so yeah, my knee, back, elbow hit on the way down and yep, instantaneously I hurt. On the more subtle emotional levels we can also feel the pain of constant negative dialogue running in the background—our thoughts of doubt, insecurity, unworthiness, negativity. Left unattended they end up reflected in our body too. The stomach aches I had—fear, stress, anxiety, mine and others in my family too, all felt in our stomachs. It was too much for me to digest, I couldn't break it down and it provided no nutritional value. My back aches I felt were a lack of a strong foundation, a lack of trust in my world and in others to give me what I needed. Lacking confidence, conviction, not knowing myself, my purpose or talents all left me aching for stability, consistency, direction and the ability to stand strong on my own.

The energy of emotions can be thought of as fuel for your car. You're supposed to use it to help you move along in life. Emotions are meant to be felt and observed, acknowledged, learned from and then let go. Like waves lapping up to the shore, emotions come in and go out. We wouldn't chase after the gas emissions from our car to put it back in and we wouldn't chase after that wave to try to keep it on the shore. Not only is it physically impossible, it's not practical. Allow those emotions coming into your body to inform you, fuel you by learning from them, and then lessons learned, let them go.

When we were younger, we had emotions that stayed in our body because we didn't know what to do with them. Children process their experiences through play. Children won't know how to manage their emotions. They play out experiences and they act them out. Children's behaviors communicate what they are feeling when they don't have the words. Most of us are not only processing current emotions but these younger ones are coming along with them too.

There will likely be some resistance as you begin to open these floodgates. At times it might feel like you are in for a tsunami to move through your body. The alternative is to stay the same, collecting emotions, until the dam breaks and you are in crisis, seemingly caught off guard.

As I sat by the pool watching my kids swim in our backyard, the world around me was turning gray. Even though it was sunny, I could only see a pinhole of sunshine coming through. I was now the smallest weight I had ever been, even though I was eating normally, but I was not keeping the weight on my bones. I was shedding a lifetime of who I had come to know I was. And I was thinking, if I was not this who was I? I was leaping into the darkness of the unknown and my body was shaking with fear. All my emotions from a lifetime of doubts, and failures were coming out. During this time I was making life-altering decisions. The sacrifices I was making were more than the rewards and I was in darkness uncovering so much information that no longer applied in order to try to find myself. I would dream of a day that these tears would be done and like a dewy morning would instead be a feeling of completeness, a sense of renewal, freshness and growth. The smell of the leaves of the creosote bush as you rub them between your fingers.

I was in the process of shedding old thought patterns and ways of being in the world, I began to experience very intense headaches frequently all day. These headaches would be a constant as I went about my day taking care of my children, attending classes, and running the house. I finally went to my physician who ordered an MRI but not after asking me if there were any events happening in my life. I didn't understand why he would ask me something so personal. How could my body, my headaches, have anything to do with all that was happening in my life? I was fine, considering. I realized I wouldn't have been able to find words, let alone the courage to tell him all that I was thinking or feeling. My experience up to that point with talking about my thoughts and feelings was that they were dismissed at the least or met with anger or hard silence.

I was in the loop of looking outside of myself for validation and approval. I knew my life changes were not being met with approval that the people I knew felt right about judging me. I began to realize that as much as I was feeling, I was still internalizing all my feelings. The MRI showed nothing physically wrong, and so his question stayed with me, and I began to see a therapist more regularly. My head ached trying to wrap my mind around all the new thoughts, emotions and information, the paradigm shift I was facing.

SUMMARY

In this chapter you are being introduced to body awareness, understanding what your body is trying to tell you. The exercises below will help you to grow your own body awareness and coupled with Chapter Two's experiments you will begin to build your dictionary of definitions. "When I have this sensation in my body, I am thinking and feeling this."

EXPERIMENT #4

HEAR YOUR BODY'S MESSAGES

Your body is giving you messages all the time, moment to moment. Your body is a reflection of your emotions. Tune into this emotional body. Your body at its natural state does not feel anything. Really! What is your body telling you?

What aches or pains, discomfort, do you have or have you had?

Was your body using a metaphor to get you to listen to a deeper meaning?

Find a place and time to lay down and close your eyes. Listen to your outer world. What do you hear, or smell? Then move into your body and listen to your inner world. What sensations do you feel? What aches, pains or discomforts? Observe your body.

I hear....

I feel....

I smell....

Put a piece of chocolate or your favorite treat in your mouth and focus on the taste, the texture, the smell, and notice everything you experience.

Sit for a few minutes to just breathe. Take natural breaths in and out and notice the sensations in your lungs and belly. Notice if you have shallow or deep breaths, long or short, deep, rough or smooth, changing or steady. Notice the difference in your body when you inhale and exhale. How does your breath feel when it leaves?

Breath into any pain, discomfort or an area of your body and Breath into that part of your body. Imagine that you are sending more oxygen to that part of your body. If you have a physical response to anxiety, stress or other emotion, tune into that part of your body and breathe into that body part, care for that body part.

Notes:

_____

_____

_____

_____

_____

_____

EXPERIMENT #5

MOVE YOUR BODY

If we hold our body tight enough we learn we can't feel. Our muscles get tight with the tension, we become inflexible and stuck in postures that can create discomforts. Dismantle the walls of the dam, push your body to slowly loosen its grip on protecting these emotions that will overflow someday if they haven't started to seep out already. When I began to learn yoga, I took a class that broke down each pose and we would practice these poses one by one. Each day I felt my body in ways that I had not felt before. As I experienced the different poses, I opened to emotions that sweetly flowed out. Along with strengthening my core and learning to stack my back, I learned how even though I felt I was standing straight, I was in fact leaning forward into the future. When I would lean back, I was then straight. This made me contemplate how I was avoiding the past. Each day as I did each pose, one by one, I felt my heart breaking open a bit more. In cobra or upward-facing dog pose. my shoulders pushed back, my back arched, my chest pushing out, a position counter to how I had been bent inward protecting my heart.

As I moved into unused muscles and challenged my normal way of holding my body, the emotions moved up and out and through. Like waves lapping up to the shore, they washed back out.

Find a way to move your body in new ways, whether it is simple stretches, a full-on dance class, or taking a walk. As you move your body, day-by-day notice the changes you feel. Is your body getting stronger? How does moving your body shift your emotions and your thoughts? As you move, feel the places in your body where you meet resistance or stiffness, and slowly challenge your body to release. Listen to the emotions that come out when you release. Let each moment pass into the next moment and look for nothing and feel everything. Suspend your mind, feel only your body, listen only to your body.

Notes:

_____

_____

_____

_____

_____

_____

EXPERIMENT # 6

THE BODY'S ENERGY

All bodies have energy vortexes, swirling energy coming from major centers of our inner body. This inner energy moves out into the world. You may recognize them as chakras. Each chakra holds an emotion, an intention and a purpose for your emotional body and your physical body. Each chakra has a vibration which can be translated into sound, color and shape.

The first chakra is located at the base of the spine. Its element is earth, its color is red, its energetic representation is grounding translated as root support.

The second chakra is located just below the belly button. Its element is water, its color is orange, its energetic representation is creativity, pleasure and emotions translated as "one's own place in life".

The third chakra is located in the solar plexus in the abdomen, its element is fire, its color is yellow, its energetic representation is power and strength of will.

The fourth chakra is located near your heart and expands down your arms and hands, its element is air, its color is green, its energetic representation is love translated as "unstuck or unhurt".

The fifth chakra is located in the throat, its element is sound, its color is bright blue, its energetic representation is expression translated as purification – meaning that the release of sound purifies and orders the energy body for entry into higher consciousness.

The sixth chakra is located in the center of the forehead. Its element is light, its color is indigo, its energetic representation is seeing the way translated as perceive and to command. The seventh chakra is located at the crown of the head. Its element is thought, its color is violet to white, its energetic representation is realization translated as thousandfold referring to the infinite unfolding.

Consider your energy.

As you reflect on these statements below, make notes. Energy is always moving, fluctuating, changing and transforming. The more we tune into it the more we learn how to manage it.

The Mandala of Mindfulness looks at each of the 7 chakras and asks you to reflect on how you are doing currently in your life with regard to each chakra quality. Place a dot for each answer to the corresponding question into the pie representing that chakra. Your goal is to have a nice round tire to roll along in life. If you see dips and divots or bulges it will be a harder ride and take more or your energy.

Mandala of Mindfulness

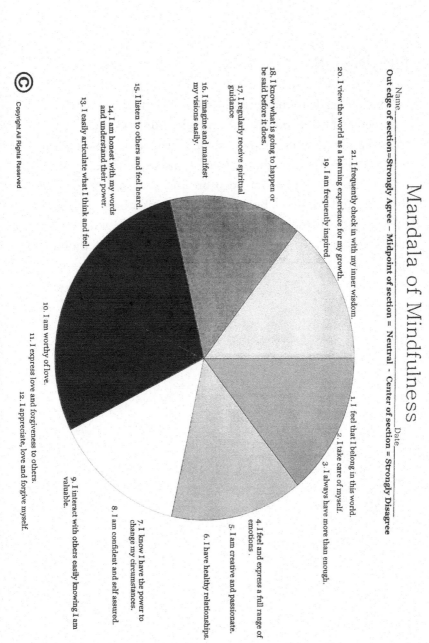

Name_____ Date_____

Out edge of section=Strongly Agree – Midpoint of section = Neutral – Center of section = Strongly Disagree

21. I frequently check in with my inner wisdom.

20. I view the world as a learning experience for my growth.

19. I am frequently inspired.

18. I know what is going to happen or be said before it does.

17. I regularly receive spiritual guidance

16. I imagine and manifest my visions easily.

15. I listen to others and feel heard.

14. I am honest with my words and understand their power.

13. I easily articulate what I think and feel.

10. I am worthy of love.

11. I express love and forgiveness to others.

12. I appreciate, love and forgive myself.

1. I feel that I belong in this world.

2. I take care of myself.

3. I always have more than enough.

4. I feel and express a full range of emotions .

5. I am creative and passionate.

6. I have healthy relationships.

7. I know I have the power to change my circumstances.

8. I am confident and self assured.

9. I interact with others easily knowing I am valuable.

MOVING ON

You will be ready to move on from this chapter when you have completed these experiments and felt your body and began to make connections with how you gain and deplete your energy, how your thoughts and emotions are reflected in your body. When you take your deep breaths, not only catch your thoughts and emotions but tune into how your body is feeling. Breathe into stiffness, pain, or discomfort. Build your dictionary by asking yourself: "Is this sensation a result of a thought or feeling?

CHAPTER FIVE:

THOUGHTS, EMOTIONS AND BEHAVIORS

A LL EMOTIONS COME FROM A THOUGHT. THE THOUGHT created your emotional response that your body is now feeling. There might have been a series of thoughts, images, or memories that were strung together in quick succession, which your brain, at lightning speed, categorized into association and patterns from the past. Begin to make connections and sense of your world. What did your body decide to feel in response to your experiences? Is there a pattern of response, "I always feel this way when..." It may feel familiar, so familiar, and normal, that we dismiss it, minimize it, ignore it. The challenge in this experiment is to not ignore the emotion you are feeling. This may get overwhelming at first because we might not have been attending to these emotions for some time.

The thing is, when we ignore them, they don't go away, we hold them in our body. This is a survival tactic of your body and a coping strategy.

Think about it. Think about when you are in a high stress situation. For example, imagine a panther is chasing you. Your body does not need to do anything but send blood and adrenaline to your legs to run to safety. It's not going to stop and think, "What am I thinking right now? or "What am I feeling?" Nope, it would be better to send all the resources into running to safety. The problem is, when I was feeling anxious as I drove from one appointment to a meeting I was not being chased by a panther. And yet, my body was having the same anxiety response. It just wasn't necessary!

The science part to note here is the relationship between the cortex and the amygdala. The amygdala is always watching to see what the cortex is thinking, ever alert to if it needs to react. The amygdala doesn't think—it just reacts. It's the primitive part of the brain that goes into fight, flight or freeze and sets up associations from the cortex. It reacts fast. Imagine you are hiking along a wooded path and you see something ahead of you that you thought looked like a snake. Your amygdala, reacting to that thought of a snake, would immediately go into a fight, flight or freeze response. Meanwhile, the cortex would say, "well wait a minute I'm not sure, let me get a bit closer." The amygdala might calm down a bit at that point but would be alert to any incoming news flash.

As you get a bit closer you see that it really was a stick in the path and not a snake. Your amygdala backs off, no emergency here. Our amygdalae cannot be trusted. It reacts without thinking, it doesn't think—it feels. Now the next time you are walking on a path and see what you think might be a snake, the amygdala will not react as quickly because of the other experience. Your cortex might not even fully believe it is a snake yet either. A new category, that sometimes a stick looks like a snake, has been created. The process of rewiring your neurotransmitters is that you will need to be in the emotional state at some level to provide it a new category and a new experience.

We can conjure emotions just by thinking of past events or feared future ones. Our thoughts and the images they produce are powerful. Thought energy is where everything that is in our world has started. When I was a child I used to take my mind to a time when my parents would be gone. I would feel their absence so intensely from my imagination that I would cry. I could feel my chest tighten, and my stomachache as I imagined that they would no longer be in my life.

Emotions stay in the body if we ignore them. This means that over time we might cry "for no reason," have a panic attack "out of the blue," or have an emotion that "just doesn't make sense." Emotions get blocked in our energy vortexes, drain our energy, and throw it out of balance. When we hold onto past emotions, they will come out sideways and they will often be bigger than we can manage. They will not necessarily be directly related to the actual events taking place in the moment. You might have even told yourself or been told that you were, "overreacting, being dramatic" or to "just calm down." When we have a passionate response to anything, know that there is a "backstory." In the Harry Potter series, there is a character "Lord Voldemort" however, no one speaks his name, instead they call him "He who must not be named." By not naming him everyone stands in great fear of him, and his power grows. Once they begin to call him by his name, once they begin to learn more about him and his backstory they understand him, his power decreases, they learn what he is likely thinking, and they learn how to manage and eventually defeat him.

Emotions help us understand what we were thinking. And we want to understand the backstory. Now you might say to me, "no, Joe over there in his speeding car made me feel angry."

Nope, your thoughts about Joe speeding past you created your emotion of anger and fear and surprise.

All thought is energy, emotions take that energy out into the world through our behaviors. Sometimes we don't even know we had an emotion until we are acting it out in our behaviors. If our emotions go unchecked, our body just needs to get involved. Your body is the last to report and, "the buck stops here." Now, you *must* notice, right?

Well…we often even ignore these messages. You might be asking yourself, "Why do I act this way?" Or people might be telling you or responding in fear because you yell, hit, throw, shut down, sulk, go silent, panic, shake, sweat, faint, can't breathe or talk. These experiences might be what brought you to this book. You might be someone who has had negative consequences to your behaviors, law enforcement, substance interventions, medical crisis, missing out on a good job or relationship. Or you might be someone who has tried to modify your body's response on your own through mellowing yourself out with drugs, alcohol, or other distractions—phones, games, work. All in attempts to not feel the feelings you are feeling. All of these coping strategies help you to dismiss your body's last resort of telling you that there is something in it that needs to be felt. Perfect! Right?

Well…. "How's that working for you?"

So at this point you might be saying to me, "But my emotions are so big and my behaviors scare me, I am doing this to protect myself and others around me." Yep, this is a noble reason to stuff 'em. And to this, I have to say, it is your responsibility to manage yourself, and no one else can do it for you. And though outside forces may try, in the end only you can truly understand you, only you know what you know. You have created a protective strategy against emotions. And the very thing that you are protecting is slowly snuffing you out.

I believe this results in the body's response to eventual bigger physical concerns like a shutdown of our immune systems, effects in blood cells, muscles, tendons, or respiratory systems and central nervous systems, weight loss or gain, stomach aches or headaches. I want you also to know that I understand the reason behind your defenses. Your defenses started as a survival response. remember? It was your body's best guess to keep you alive. But we are more than our body. I believe we are a soul in a human body. We need to understand and learn about the body in order to manage it and be in charge of the body instead of it being in charge of us.

SUMMARY

This chapter focuses only on shining a light on your emotions. By doing the experiments below you will learn how to name them, how to express them and how to manage them.

EXPERIMENT #7

EMOTIONS IN THE BODY

When you check in to identify your emotions, feel your body—where does this emotion live in your body? Look at the body outline below, make copies of it so that you can do this for all your emotions. At the top of the page write the one emotion you are experiencing, then take a color that represents the emotion, locate where in your body you are feeling it and color the shape that it might have on the location of your body.

Then take a deep breath and feel the emotion. Take as many deep breaths as you need until you feel that emotion leave your body. At the bottom of your emotional body page write out what you were thinking.

I want to be able to walk up to you at any moment and ask you: "What are you thinking and how do you feel about that?"

When you decide to start something, a project, a job hunt, dating, or even dinner, what do you say to yourself, what are you thinking and feeling?

When you are at a social event, or out in public or even just thinking about going out, what are you saying to yourself, what are you thinking and feeling?

When you are stressed out, something has gone wrong, the baby's crying too much, the dog is annoying you to go out, it's too loud, too chaotic, there are too many chores, there are dirty dishes in the sink, there are no clean clothes, you can't get all your work done at your job, you partner is upset with you, what do you say to yourself, what are you thinking and feeling?

Notes:

_____

_____

_____

_____

_____

1

EXPERIMENT #8

IDENTIFY HOW YOU ACT WHEN YOU HAVE AN EMOTION

Look at the outline of your body and identify what you did to express the emotions on the page or what you felt like doing to express them. What behaviors did you choose to express your emotions? Take a deep breath and find the space in which you have not acted on your emotion but that you have a choice. You may say to yourself "I feel this way and could express it by doing this or by doing this." Or you could even just acknowledge that you are experiencing this emotion and you do not have to express it in a behavior at all. Consider and tune into the thought patterns that created your emotions. Try shifting your thoughts and watch as your emotion shifts.

Notes:

_____

_____

_____

_____

_____

_____

_____

MOVING ON

You will be ready to move on to the next chapter when you have completed the experiments of learning what you are feeling and where you feel it in your body as well as identifying how you express your emotions and how you want to express your emotions.

CHAPTER SIX:

NEGATIVE THOUGHTS

B Y NOW, HOPEFULLY YOU HAVE ESTABLISHED A STRONG practice of breathing and catching your thoughts and feelings. You might feel quite miserable hearing all the negative messages you say to yourself. I know I did. In fact, my discovery took many years. I did not have a guide to give it to me straight, to help me connect the dots. I have had to piece it all together from comments and experiences over my life to fully understand.

On one particular morning, I was dressed for an interview, in my skirt suit I recently bought from Brooks Brothers, hose, high heels, and ironed blouse, nervous, sweating through my sleeves. Searching for an address, as I walked along the uneven sidewalks in downtown Kansas City, I was walking fast, anxiously thinking, how many interviews have I been on? Thousands. But I looked the part. Look good, that was a strong message that I received all my life. The appearance that all was fine. There is a photo when I was five with a perm in my naturally straight hair. Later when I grew it out mom would call it stringy. I began wearing glasses when I was in third grade and got braces shortly after that. With my braces finally off, I wanted contacts to improve my look. My dad said that he liked my glasses better. Later when I was in my 20s, I finally got the courage to ask him if he thought I was pretty he stated that, "I was interesting-looking." Not the answer I was expecting but it did explain why I never considered myself pretty. My world reflected my flaws. My nose turned up, my cheek bones too high, too tall, too skinny, pigeon-toed, don't arch your back, you don't take criticism well, stubborn, reduce yourself, modify, smile more, act dumb.

My first year out of college was during the Regan-era recession. While others around me were seemingly landing white-collar jobs, and my childhood friend had a job lined up through her dad, she and I traveled off to live in Minneapolis,I hit roadblock after roadblock with my bachelor's degree. It seemed to warrant no merit. While sitting in one interview for a graphic design position, the white male interviewer commented that he was surprised I hadn't landed a job since I was so pretty. After one more interview for a graphic design position, I received a call from the young man who had interviewed me. He said he couldn't offer me a position but would like to take me out on a date. I took what I was offered. I accepted the date, no longer challenging the feedback given to me. I dated him the longest I had ever dated anyone, until he, too, broke up with me. Hearing the break-up news over the phone, I hung up and hit the closest thing to me, a metal picture frame hanging on my wall.. It slashed my wrist and I slid down onto the hardwood floor looking at the cut, thinking about killing myself. In Minneapolis I had so many failures, it seems I was set up to fail. With much desperation and frustration after hundreds of interviews I pieced together $12,000 in income that first year out of college as a waitress, key liner, editor, and photographer. One day I answered an ad in the paper that only asked "Do you want a fun job?" I was ready for fun by now and thoroughly defeated so I answered the ad and got the job as a rental car agent at the Minneapolis St. Paul International airport.

One night I was in the basement of my apartment complex sorting through my storage space to get my bike hung, when all of a sudden, boxes tumbled down on top and around me knocking me into the side of the unit, putting me in a daze for a few minutes. I sat on the floor shocked, afraid and then I cried. I didn't just cry about getting hit by boxes. What a metaphor for my life then! I felt alone and beat down, literally. I decided to leave my job at a rental car agency and move to Kansas City, to go home.

But I was going to get a job before I moved. I didn't want to repeat the endless job search I had gone through in Minneapolis. And I set out to Kansas City to find one. I lined up interviews and places to stay, but before I even left the city I lost my wallet at the gas stop. I didn't realize it until I arrived at my hotel in Iowa and instead of bubble bath and a good night's sleep, I called an old boyfriend who lived there, and he let me stay at a house he was watching. There was no food in the house that I was allowed to have and of course he made sexual advances which fell flat. I snuck out of the empty house alone in the morning. A few hours later, I made it to the loop outside of Kansas City. I just kept going around and around looking for the exit to my college roommate's house.

Stuck in a loop, that too sounded metaphoric.

Hours later, I finally arrived. I was exhausted. This trip was off to a bad start. I should have seen the roadblocks as signs that you can't go back. I was stubborn and set to implement my plan no matter what signs got in my way. I persevered, and

I hoped for an easy transition into a position at the Kansas City rental car agency since I had been a valued worker in Minneapolis. The hiring manager picked me up from a hotel parking lot as a halfway point and we talked in her office. She had no positions. I was confused but she said that another rental car agency might be hiring, and she booked me with the hiring manager that same day. I was hopeful. She dropped me off and I waited, when I finally was able to meet with this man, I realized that this didn't feel like a real interview, and he never talked about positions or availability. Late now in the day, he suggested drinks, if the hiring manager who brought me would come. During drinks and then dinner, I realized they were a couple when they decided to call a guy to join us and I had been used as a cover or excuse. Now I was on a double date and though I was asking to be taken back to my car, they insisted that this guy could take me to my car. He took me to his apartment, and when I insisted, he finally took me to the hotel parking lot to my car. Tired from a long unproductive day and still trying to present as everything was all good, no problems, don't make waves, don't speak up. I wasn't too surprised when he thought that I was staying at that hotel and he was going to get a hookup. Defeated, lost, alone, again.

Loneliness won in the end and I moved without a job that year.

Now I'm plowing down the street to another interview. I'm holding my keys between my fingers, even though it's daylight, I am a woman. I'm practically running in high heels to get to the next interview. I couldn't even tell you who this interview was with. I whizzed by a man who was walking along at a normal pace, and he yelled out after me, "You sound like a horse!" I finally hired an employment agency to help me find a job and soon got hired for a position answering phones and stuffing envelopes at the Board of Trade. After mixing up letters meant for other people, and not smiling in the elevator, I moved on to try a job in sales. I had no experience in answering phones and stuffing letters and I had no experience in sales either. I worked hard, getting contacts, making sales pitches, hoping I'd reach my quota each week, each month. I was lousy at this compared to my colleagues who seemed to get sales so effortlessly. I tried to learn from them, attempting strategies they used and working even harder. My company sent me to a Dale Carnegie Sales Talk course and with the help of one of the instructors I won the Sales Talk championship for my class. I was hopeful and so I bought a new car, a new light-blue Mazda, I bought a four-door because I thought that someday I'd like to get married and have kids and this would allow for kids to be in the back. Never mind that I wasn't dating anyone at the moment. I was paying on the car monthly, to my dad, because as a woman, I couldn't get a car loan or even buy a car on my own. This was back when you ordered cars and waited for them to come in. I had asked for a light-blue car with light-blue interior, when it came in I excitedly drove off the lot.

In better light, I suddenly realized that the interior wasn't light blue at all, instead it was gray. I circled back around to the dealership. I pointed this out to the sales manager who argued with me. All of the rejection from my past experiences just made me more stubborn. I stood firm and insisted that I get what I had ordered. The salesman that had helped me buy the car stood by silently, not offering any support or validating my order. Instead he slipped a note into my hand and indicated that I should not let anyone know. I left without my car that day and as I read the note from the salesman it merely said that he respected me for standing up for what I wanted. Life to me seemed to be a constant series of ups and downs, compromises, adapting and just making what was dealt to me be okay.

I took my new car with the blue interior on my new sales calls, and I was starting to get into a routine. It was hard work though and I never felt at ease. I remember one day on the last day of the month and I needed just one more sale to make my quota, I had several appointments lined up none of which resulted in a signed contract so far. On the last call of the day, this sale had to come through for me to meet my quota. I left that meeting crushed when they turned me down. My mind was furiously thinking about what else I could do, who else I could call to meet that quota, right now! As reality slowly sunk in and I began to accept that I was out of options, I took the exit off the freeway to my apartment in my new, beautiful blue Mazda, where I lived alone. Tears rolled down my face. I was a failure, again. I glanced around at the other drivers worried they would see me and worried what they would think of me. That evening alone in my apartment the negative messages mounted, one stacked on the next as I reviewed my entire life with supporting evidence that my belief that I was not good enough was definitely true.

I dated a guy briefly during the time I had this job, and he was in sales too. The difference was that he was successful. I remember one thing he said to me about sales which I see now can be applied to everything. He said, the more you try to grab mercury, the more it scatters. My anxiety and pressure to succeed was creating desperation in everything I did. I was so anxious, so caught in my mind, I never stopped trying to figure things out, push through, persevere, reach perfection, do it right, be right, look right, say all the right things, all the while a running background of negative thoughts dragging me down.

I had one foot on the gas pedal and the other foot on the brakes. I didn't see it at the time, this was my normal and it was getting increasingly uncomfortable and unforgiving. I knew things weren't right, but, maybe if I did this or that, if I got a boyfriend or a sale, then things would be okay. And the regrets, why did I leave Minneapolis where at least I had a job. I started to really understand the concept that wherever you go, there you are.

One day I came into my sales job, and I felt a tense, fearful, heaviness in the office. I didn't know what I was feeling was energy at the time, I didn't know anything about energy, or feeling things that other people were feeling or thinking. But I got that all too familiar pit in my stomach—fear. And my interpretation was that I had done something wrong—again. I took it on for my own, and I knew at that moment that I was going to be fired. Yep, I was laid off. A failure, again. I eventually got another job building picture frames. My first job when I was 15 was building frames. So, this was my default kind of job, the job I would quickly go back to in a pinch. When I was 15, every Saturday and after school I would ride my bike to the frame shop. My boss was very intimidating, and I would freeze in fear of her. My faults would then inevitably shine in light of these fears. The sizes of frames, mats and glass were all figured out by hand back then, using simple math. My mind flashed back to third grade standing at the board in front of the whole class doing math equations, my dad getting visibly frustrated when I asked questions about high school math. In fear, I froze. My boss at the Kansas City frame shop would literally scream at me for not knowing how to do something—assuming I had been trained by his other employees. On my lunch breaks I would drive to the closest park and sit in my car and cry.

I was adopted when I was a couple months old and often messages to myself would include the theme that I wasn't supposed to be born, that I was unwanted in the world and didn't really belong, didn't have a real family. I would think that I should have been aborted, and I would be angry thinking that abortion would have been the kinder thing to have done with my life.

During intensely defeating moments, I would pile on previous life events from my school days and all the thoughts and beliefs I held. I didn't know it at the time, but that is just what the mind does, make associations. "Oh", the mind will say, "we're thinking about this horrible feeling, we'll remember these." And then throw them all into a big vessel—my body. Flashes of memories of other boyfriends who didn't come to the phone, broke up with me, used me, times when I didn't make the drill team, not being included, invited, asked out, left out, left behind, lost jobs, failing jobs, not getting jobs, the theme of rejecting and being alone, always alone. I felt so bad.

I learned early on that alcohol helped, a lot. It numbed the pain for a time. In fact I even felt happy when I would drink a glass or two of beer or wine. It was my go-to when I felt bad or socially awkward and wanted to fit in with the cool kids. Later, much later, I would make a rule that when I felt bad I couldn't drink. And eventually, I stopped drinking and doing lots of other things I realized my body didn't need to have including holding on to old beliefs and thought patterns. For most of my life through my 20s, I was drifting along, being tugged in whatever direction there seemed to be something I could grab onto, that might save me.

When I got the last job I would have in Kansas City, it was due in a large part by knowing the human resources director at the company. It was at a larger company and my mom was so proud of me she came to visit with a friend.

Ahh, I guess this was the meaning of success, was I finally doing something right?

All through that day, I would be barraged by constant doubts. The other women who had applied for the job and didn't believe that I could possibly be right for the position, spread rumors and I was shunned by the staff. Alone, again. But I was learning, and my manager was teaching me and supporting me and encouraging me. His words were so different from any words I had ever heard. I was feeling what it might feel like to achieve career advancement, to be given opportunities—well perhaps not as many as my younger white male colleagues—but for me... my bar was pretty low. I was proud and exhausted by the end of every day. At this time I also met the man I would marry. In short, life was great, finally! He was an eagle scout and worked in the stock market industry, both things my parents would surely admire. At my wedding, my mom was the happiest I had ever seen her. "Ok, now I am making progress," I thought "I have a job and a husband she is proud of. I have done something 'right.'"

What I didn't realize was I had really just reached another dead end—I had run out of options. I was once again grabbing at straws, taking what was presented to me. When all else failed I had eventually turned to following a formula of what was expected of me, get a job in a big company, marry a solid guy, please my mother.

Negative thoughts get in the way of living your best life.

Negative thoughts come from all those voices who raised us, from all the experiences we have in the world. One negative thought feed on the next. We set up a world that attracts and reflects these thoughts. Negative thoughts also come from beliefs that we hold. We say something to and about ourselves long enough and we begin to believe it. We say something long enough and it is reflected back to us and we say, "see? It's true!" We are now caught in a loop. A very painful loop of never getting what we want or need and always getting the same result. We think we are doing things differently, as though this time, we will push through, but it always turns out the same.

Words are powerful, they begin with thoughts and thought energy holds the same power. How we are treated reflects the intention of words unspoken. My seven-year-old daughter was explaining this concept to me the other day when she was telling me about a friend who was angry and frustrated with her. My daughter used her body to "tell" how she knew her friend was angry. She showed me examples of rolling the eyes, crossing the arms, turning her back, turning her head and stomping her feet.

Words and thoughts set up a power as strong as any curse. Know that your words and thoughts to yourself can be just as powerful. We learn these types of responses early in our lives, from parents who model their own levels of managing their thoughts and feelings: never fighting, ignoring bad behavior, shushing us, yelling, shutting down. We keep learning them throughout our lives. The good news is, we can re-learn and unlearn. When we grow up not witnessing examples of talking through difficult conversations we don't know how. When we don't hear revelations of how others feel we don't have the words to articulate them for ourselves and we don't know how to manage them. When we are ignored and shushed, we don't feel we can speak up and sometimes we stop trying.

When I was in my 40s I attended an I Ching meditation retreat, we would study the I Ching during the day and then go into silence until the following day after breakfast and meditation. One day, as the instructor was asking for ideas about a ceremony we were planning, I raised my hand and at his nod began to speak. The woman sitting next to me quickly whipped her hand across my mouth. I was shocked and as I looked around the room at the other women they were shaking their heads and looking away. What had I missed? The instructor came over to my seat, standing over me, as I struggled to process the subtle (and not so subtle) information coming in at me. He demanded I say what I was going to say. With my voice shaking and trying not to cry, I fought against a lifetime of being shushed, and I crunched out my thoughts. The group was immediately dismissed, and I was left with the instructor and organizers to process what just happened. The instructor sternly blamed me and told me that I needed to speak up for myself.

To this day I am still unclear why my group believed that I should not speak. My sense was that their knowledge of the instructor from past groups was that he didn't really want any ideas to be brought forward and they were trying to warn me of potential rath from him. After a group photo before we headed to our cars to leave, I turned and thanked the instructor. His face showed the shock at my appreciation, as if I shouldn't be thanking him after how I was treated.

These events can live on in our minds, playing repeatedly until you believe the negative thought about yourself. Eventually, you take it on for your own voice, your own truth. Think of these words and actions as our "villains," and in order to defeat them we need to know who they are, to name them. And we need to muster up our superpowers of detection to overcome the repeated attacks. When I cried in my car driving home from my last sales appointment, I wasn't just crying because I didn't meet my quota, I was crying because I was thinking I had failed again, like so many times, I was feeding on my experiences of never getting it right. When I cried in shame for trying to speak up in a group, I was replaying unspoken beliefs that I did not have anything of value to say, that I was wrong.

SUMMARY

This chapter introduced the way our brains hold on to negative memories, events, and experiences, in flashes, moments and fleeting comments even, and how our brains pull them forward into our present-day lives. The experiments below will help you to learn how to identify and manage these thoughts.

EXPERIMENT #8

THE EMOTIONAL POWER OF WORDS

With the list you created in **"Experiment #3—Identify the emotion you are feeling"** from the third chapter, identify the root of the messages. One by one, name the emotion and reflect on the questions below.

Name of the Emotion

_____

_____

_____

_____

Where have you heard this message before?

_____

_____

_____

_____

What familiar feeling in your body goes along with this message?

_____

_____

_____

What past events that come flashing to your mind?

_____

_____

_____

_____

_____

Name of the Emotion

_____

_____

_____

_____

Where have you heard this message before?

_____

_____

_____

_____

What familiar feeling in your body goes along with this message?

_____

_____

_____

_____

What past events that come flashing to your mind?

_____

_____

_____

_____

Name of the Emotion

_____

_____

_____

_____

Where have you heard this message before?

_____

_____

_____

_____

What familiar feeling in your body goes along with this message?

_____

_____

_____

_____

What past events that come flashing to your mind?

_____

_____

_____

_____

EXPERIMENT #9

CHALLENGE THE NEGATIVE MESSAGES

The way the mind functions could be thought of characteristically like the mind of a four-year old. Just like a four-year-old, your mind has no filter, it thinks and thinks about the same things over and over. Just like a four-year-old, the mind will move from one topic to another by way of associations being reminded of one thing or another. You are not four-years old, but like a four-year old your mind is very demanding, "look at me, watch me, listen to me."

Sometimes these thoughts can be pretty dramatic. Often these thoughts are determined to prove to you that they are absolutely right. Needless to say, your four-year-old mind needs a benevolent, loving, wise parent—you , to provide structure and guidance. You would not let a four-year-old run out into the street, stay up late or even go on and on saying the same thing over and over. No, you would kindly tell that four-year-old that for their safety we don't run out of the house and when we cross a street we look both ways, that we need our sleep and so we help them get ready for bed. We help them relax and we stay with them until they fall asleep, we set up a routine that they can count on and we remind them of the task currently at hand. And you would redirect that four-year-old when they have said the same thing 100 times, letting them know that you heard them, but now we are getting dressed, or getting ready to do this or that.

Likewise, we must do this with our mind's thoughts. Now that you have a handle on what you are saying and why you are saying these things to yourself, it's time to manage them. It's time to free up your headspace. No more running amuck without discipline.

On one side of your paper write out one of your negative thoughts you have discovered you say to yourself. For example—"I'm a failure, I never do anything right, I messed up, I'm no good" Across from this thought, write out what you would say to this thought if you were talking kindly to a child trying to provide reason, structure, encouragement and support and give them a better, more positive direction. For example,

- "I have accomplished ____"
- "I completed _____"
- "I am proud that I _____"
- "That's just not true."
- "It's okay"
- "I'm learning"
- "I'll do better next time"
- "I learned ____."

Negative Thoughts	Benevolent Response

EXPERIMENT #10

REPLACE NEGATIVE THOUGHTS

By now you have done a lot of research into your thoughts, feelings and behaviors and likely have some idea of what you *don't* want to be thinking any more. But nature hates a void and it's the same for your mind. It wants to think but it really doesn't care what it thinks. And so, it will think what it always thinks unless we give it something new. The mind will default to the thoughts you first learned, or the ones that were the most upsetting, or the ones that you are used to thinking. With intention and the power of knowing your themes, you create a new thought to insert into your mind.

When I first started therapy we created a statement for my mind to turn to when it was spinning. My new statement or Mantra was "I rise above it all and live and love happily." And I imagined I was in a hot air balloon, getting a better perspective and feeling safe.

What would you rather be thinking?

_____

_____

What would you rather be feeling?

_____

_____

Replacement thought

_____

_____

Begin to commit to a regular routine of deep breathing, and catching your thoughts, feelings and actions. Label those thoughts, identify those emotions and with your new replacement thought, confidently state with conviction your new one liner.

MOVING ON

You will be ready to move on to the next chapter once you have identified the emotion that your thought created, when you have challenged your thoughts and replaced the negative messages with a new thought or mantra to say to instead.

CHAPTER SEVEN:

MORE THOUGHTS ON THOUGHTS

GROWING UP IN A RELIGIOUS FAMILY, I LEARNED TO PRAY A certain way and it included a lot of talking, asking, pleading, wishing, hoping as well as thankfulness for our food and then Amen. Prayer occurred only at a church service or before a meal. Though I got the concept that God was always there, I didn't have the sense of that presence.

I remember sitting on a grassy hill at a church retreat with other high schoolers at sunset waiting for that sense, and watching the sun go down with anticipation that maybe I would feel—something profound, without even knowing what that feeling would be. I rarely felt anything but perhaps anxiety and fear and was ever hopeful to feel what I thought would be close to happiness.

As I got older, my times attending church services were rarer. When I did attend, sitting in a quiet church service, emotion would begin to rise and after several frantic minutes trying desperately to hold them in had failed, tears would roll down my cheeks. At the time I didn't look at what I was thinking or identify what emotions were behind the tears. Then the service would end. I tucked everything back in and went on to the tasks in my life.

When I was raising my babies the only time I found for myself was 5:00 in the morning before my husband left for work to arrive before the stock market opened on the east coast. In Arizona, for most of the year, this was the most consistent time of day when it would be cooler, and so it worked perfectly. I was in my 30s by now and reclaiming physical exercise by way of outdoor walks turned out to be good for my mental health as well. I realized that I didn't want to talk to God so much at 5:00 in the morning. For me it started as just being quiet. Soon on these walks, I began to receive instead, and just like in the quiet church services, emotions would again surface. I heard the birds' songs and their fluttering for food. I felt the sun rising in the east. I smelled the grass and water from early morning sprinklers. I saw the sparkle as the sun slid in and the contrasting shadows where it didn't reach.

And I began to hear my voice.

I'd heard most of my thoughts before, so I started putting aside messages of criticism. By now they no longer fit on those peaceful walks, and instead I assured myself I was doing everything "right." I was married, had children. I had checked the boxes and I should be happy, so why the tears? I tried to make sense of my unease, acknowledging that this life I had created felt like it was never-ending and all-consuming. I had moved three times, had given birth to two children, made friends, left them, started new jobs, and left them all in the span of three years.

Being in a relationship and raising two small children was hard for me. For some reason it was slowly draining my energy, my life force. I felt the all-too-familiar depression and feeling of being trapped. Wanting to make the discomfort go away, in the past this is when I would make a change. I would place blame on others, and thought if only they would do more, be more, give me more—then I would be happy. This only led to feeling resentful, and jealous of other people's lives which appeared to move forward while mine seemed to be standing still. When I finally was able to talk about my ambiguous feelings with my husband he stated that I'd never had it so good. I couldn't hear these words as encouragement and instead didn't feel validated.

If I never had it so good, then why did I feel so bad?

On these quiet morning walks, I suspended my thoughts. They were clearly my defenses and I was coming to realize that thinking my way out of this wasn't working, I was at a loss and in my silence, I was on top of that grassy hill again waiting for—something. Something I couldn't define and therefore couldn't grasp for. As I walked, I focused on my breath and my muscles as they moved the energy through my body. Nature absorbed my chaos, and for 30 minutes I listened, I observed and let it go. I expressed gratitude and let it go, moment to moment, step-by-step, heel-to-toe, and my mind slowed down to silence.

One day on my walk, I thought back to the dream I had woken up from that morning.

I was inside of a never-ending bright white tunnel. In this dream I was calmly looking around the space which was comfortably close to my body. In this tunnel, I was engaged, alert, calm, aware, alive. These walls were the whitest white I had ever seen, and I saw the potential there in that tunnel. My mind immediately started to imagine colors and shapes and I caught these thoughts and stopped them. I thought, "don't be too quick to fill it up, slow down." I suspended the urge and instead continued to stay in the unknown. This image stayed with me for days and weeks. Each time my mind tried to imagine something on the walls, I suspended the urge. As the days rolled by, a growing sense began to come into focus and those walls remained white. I allowed the idea to emerge that I was to reclaim the nudges from long ago to be a minister.

When I allowed my mind to receive I watched as the fragments and pieces fell into place around that idea. I would somehow use my creative arts background—the one that wanted to paint on those walls—and I would somehow be in service to helping others. We had moved from California to Arizona two years before. We had a new church community and had made new friends here. I was active in my church and ran a women's group, attending and leading bible study groups and mom's groups. I was involved at the national and state level of women's events and our annual holiday fundraising. I had even been asked to create a banner to reflect an upcoming event. And while it was stressful to get two small children up and dressed for church each Sunday, we attended services regularly.

I began to research what my vague thoughts were trying to conceptualize and discovered that a job existed in the ministry that would allow this type of creativity and flexibility. I found information on pastoral counseling and felt that this was the fit. A dear friend who we left behind in California exclaimed in a phone conversation later that I had a "calling." This she defined as a God telling me what to do.

Well, it did seem like I had allowed myself to be led by spirit.

My friendship with a woman in our Arizona church community was growing to where we would talk daily. We had kids the same age and we would bring our kids together for play dates throughout the week. My friend was involved in church activities with me as well and our spiritual connection grew along with our friendship. Interestingly, around this time my friend also felt compelled to go into the ministry and we talked this over with a female minister at our church. I began the process of becoming accepted into seminary school and some months later once I was approved by the Elders of my church I was standing at a podium giving a talk about my life and stating my intentions to the larger Presbyterian body. I was voted to proceed and enrolled in seminary school to begin the next summer. My parents even gave me money for my first class. Life was going well. I had a focus, a direction. I felt I was reclaiming my purpose and heading in a direction that put all my experiences together. I was hopeful. And it was at this same time that my friend would bring me information about herself, thoughts that had been swirling in her head as she grappled with her own anxiety and depression. She talked to me about how she thought she was gay.

My mind catapulted to a memory of my family and I sitting at the Thanksgiving table along with my aunt, uncle and my three male cousins. The AIDS crisis was hitting the nation and the world at that time in the 70s, and there were many heated debates about what it was. There was misinformation, speculation and fear on all sides.

I was in high school at the time and while I can't say I even knew what a gay person was, let alone know anyone who was gay, I knew that they were humans, people just like the rest of us. My family was discussing this topic around the table that Thanksgiving, and as usual I was quiet, listening and observing. My uncle voiced the side of most Christians at this time, that AIDS was the result of sinful behavior. He called gay men faggots. My youngest cousin misheard and said, "what? maggots?" and everyone broke out into a burst of laughter to which milk then spewed from my cousins' nose. My aunt and mom jumped up from the table to grab something to clean up the mess and the topic ended.

But it never left my mind. I remember feeling concerned, curious, confused by the contradiction of the definition of love. I heard the message clearly "we" didn't approve of gay people and they were not "good." In fact, God didn't like them either and was punishing them for their behavior with AIDS. I thought back to my California friend whose brother was gay, and she told me that because of this she never let him be with her son alone and that her parents didn't speak with him and that she might have to end her relationship with him as well. I knew that if my Arizona friend was gay that I would likely have people coming to me with similar thoughts as a pastoral counselor and that I would need to know more about this. Over the days and months my friend would answer my questions about her experiences over her life that had led her to this discovery. On the Venn diagram of things, I quickly realized that her experiences reflected similar experiences of mine. This gave me pause and a growing uneasiness. I took them out one-by-one, moments in time, fleeting thoughts and snapshots of events—attraction to a girl in grade school, my need and focus to connect at emotional levels with other women. The kiss when words couldn't express my overwhelming joy and connection with a friend. The unidentified awkwardness I felt undressing in the girl's locker room.

I thought about my lack of prolonged interest in most boys or men, or even knowing or remembering that they liked me. The crushes I felt in my 20s and the daydreams of being intimate with my female boss at the rental car agency in Minneapolis.

Was it possible that these moments meant something more defined?

Something that up until now was unlabeled, undefined, and in my mind uncategorized for me to understand? Could this also be why I never felt like I fit in? Never fully satisfied, always searching for something—more? This was back before it was as simple as googling a topic so I went to the library and looked for books about being gay. I read in the aisles, afraid to check anything out, afraid to even be in the aisle. All the pieces kept falling into place, other's stories and experiences were running parallel with my own in many ways. As I wrestled with these past thoughts and memories and new thoughts and information, I realized that I had been slowly falling in love, that I was connecting with my friend because I wanted not just a friendship, but something more.

I wondered about my feelings for other girlfriends that I had and realized that I held an attraction in many of them. I stepped into the anxiety-provoking thought that perhaps she would want to be with me. I was so naive, so sheltered, I thought I knew what I was supposed to do—date guys, get married and have children. I had done this—was there something more? One day, standing at the kitchen counter grating cheese for party potatoes, I was thinking of my friend, and felt the unexpected stirring of desire electrify my entire system. Something woke in me, energy rushed through me as if a dam had been opened. As I doubled over and stopped grating that cheese, I sobbed. I was shocked and filled with awe and sadness at that same time. I had never felt this intensity with a man. The contrast was profound, and it hit me —this must be what other couples felt and why their connections were so strong.

I cried for wanting this and I cried because I didn't have it playing out in my life. I knew, in that moment and all the subsequent moments, that I too was gay. I also realized that

I could not go into the ministry as a gay person—it was not allowed. I sat in the small prayer room meant for one person at the church and I prayed. I asked God for guidance. I knew I couldn't live an incongruent life and I knew that I wanted my children to be protected. I sat in silence, my face soaked in my tears, feeling the overwhelming rush flow into me, and another piece was added to the pristine white tunnel walls. This new focus, direction and purpose was not only about a career change—it was about all of me. It slowly began to dawn on me, that if you live for others all your life you have no life. There are no scuffs on the walls, and there are no colors either. I *was* the blank wall and it seemed that now I was being pushed into a paradigm shift I knew nothing about. A pencil drawing I made during this time reflected my fear. I was naked, hanging onto a rope that had no beginning and no end, over a dark ocean of waves. The leap of faith I would take would be into the unknown and it would call on a trust in myself that I would need to nurture and grow.

Dismantling years of living one way, examining if they were ways you chose or were imposed or chosen for you. Waking up to the discovery that you have a choice and that the only thing keeping you from seeing those choices was your own thinking. At some point the choice becomes clear. I still had a choice of whether to live the full knowledge of who I discovered I was or not. It had become too painful to stay the same and expect a different result. It was too painful to try to fit into another's ideals of "right." In sessions with clients, I would hold up my notepad in front of my face and say, "you are seeing only this paper in front of you and you think this is all there is to see." But if you move your head slightly to the left, right, top, or bottom or even turn all the way around from that pad of paper, you can see that there is so much more, so many other ways of seeing beyond the paper and your present situation. We put ourselves into our own prisons, for all our reasons, and are we fully informed? Have we made conscious choices from a multitude of choices? Are they "right" for us?

Your experience may not feel as seemingly life-altering as mine, but I can assure you it will feel the same in that it will be different than anything you have known before. This work, while it might feel like a bulldozer is crashing everything, is more of an internal shift. Think of the act of panning for gold. You start off by taking large quantities from the banks of the river, you run it through a sifter, then wash away the residue, then pour out the fine silt that is left and swirl it around in your pan, looking for the smallest of flakes of gold. We are in the process of getting rid of the boulders, rocks, pebbles, and sand and looking for the gold. This process, when working with your life takes time, years perhaps—and this is the beginning.

You will need courage to continue to face the space between your thoughts and begin to listen. You will need to be brave to face your fears of your paradigm shift and do it anyway. You will need patience, though you have sifted through the big stuff and shifted to a new perspective the world around you has not changed. The sky is still there, the chair you are sitting in is the same, you are wearing the same shirt, your heart is still beating the same beat, people around you have not seemingly changed. Being in the space between thoughts you will begin to see more support around you. Look for these supports, accept them as gifts to you to continue your brave journey into truly seeing. You will also be righting past relationships that were never set up to fit who you are becoming. These relationships have a choice to grow and evolve with you. The people in your life will have an opportunity to be brave and courageous along with you or remain in their comfortable uncomfortableness without you. You might experience everything in between these two responses. Allow the people around you to be on their own journey, have their own responses to the changes you are feeling inside, and to be in their own uncomfortableness.

As I sat with my realization, I knew that I needed to bring my husband up-to-date and we began a tough conversation punctuated by hurt feelings, resentment, loss and grief. My parents learned of my paradigm shift through someone other than myself and their response was to disagree and eventually believe that they were no longer comfortable with me, that they no longer knew me and so as a consequence to their thoughts, beliefs and emotions, they created distance. My parents however, put this on me, rationalizing to themselves that I had pushed them away.

Expect these loops of reasoning that keep others in their comfort zone. This work might not be for everyone, but everyone has the opportunity. When discomfort is being experienced, know that you are on the right path, you are learning and growing. And take your time. Be thoughtful, considerate, give yourself grace. You alone, live with yourself, no one else can live for you, and likewise living for someone else will never serve you.

SUMMARY

This chapter addresses how to create more space between your thoughts, and what to do with a less-cluttered mind. The experiments below will guide you to creating space, learn how your body reacts to change and challenge you to find new ways of looking at situations.

EXPERIMENT #11

CREATING SPACE

By now you are well on your way with taking deep breaths hourly, or more often. You are catching your thoughts and making connections and little by little you are showing your mind that you are in charge. Your thoughts have likely slowed down a bit. In this experiment you will begin to show your mind why you are slowing the thoughts down, to hear the space between. To create new experiences and new thoughts to emerge, and to receive.

Pull out the learning styles chart and if you haven't already, identify the way you best learn. For me on my walks it was through movement, kinesthetic learning. While I am a visual learner as well (remember all the images I kept trying to conjure) I slowed my mind by moving. You might find that you are a combination as well. You will discover in this experiment how to create even more space between your thoughts. Start with your identified learning style and do one or more of the actives listed. Then move on to the other two learning styles and try some of the activities listed there as well. Each of these activities are designed for you to slow down and focus only on what you are doing, nothing else.

Auditory—listen to music that has no words, classical, jazz, piano, whatever you enjoy, just no words.

Visual—draw, paint, doodle, nothing too heady—meditative without expectation

---

Kinesthetic—walk, run, dance, stretch

EXPERIMENT #12

GETTING COMFORTABLE IN THE UNCOMFORTABLENESS

Your first thoughts are just your body's go-to, what it learned a long time ago. They aren't the only thoughts out there. Look beyond the pad of paper. It's time to bring in more information.

Your mind is used to patterns and likes to make patterns in response to the world. It likes to learn it and forget about it. The mind likes to learn something and go unconscious—it is basically quite lazy. When you first learn something ,the mind is all over it. Remember when you first learned to drive, hands at 10 and two, checking knobs, pedals, mirrors. Now we can drive from point A to B and not even know how we got there.

Wake up your mind.

It will rebel, it will feel uncomfortable, it won't like it. It will stomp its feet like the four-year-old self that it is and will whine and plead, "but we always do it this way!" Be the benevolent parent to your mind, reassure it, take a deep breath and suspend your thoughts.

1. BREAK A PATTERN.

Think about a pattern you have, a small one that might not even matter, break it, and feel the resistance in your body. Look at the patterns you have created in your world and choose one to break. Choose action steps that will shake up your routine. For example, when you jump into the shower I can guarantee that you wash your body the same way every time—Now, consciously and intentionally do it differently and watch your mind "freak out." Did I wash my hair yet? I don't know! Breaking a habit will require that your mind be alert, awake and engaged.

---

2. CREATE A NEW PATTERN.

Using the research data from the **Energy Input and Energy Output** from the second chapter, choose one or two new habits you would like to change. Glance at the **Stages of Change** from the second chapter as well and understand what will go into making this change and what stage you are in.

EXPERIMENT #13

THREE NEW PERSPECTIVES

When we were young we adapted, our bodies picked their best guess at what would work to keep us alive. It tucked experiences, moments, fleeting thoughts, and feelings away. We didn't need them then to survive. Now that we are older ,some of these survival techniques, the body's automatic response to situations by association, are keeping us imprisoned into thinking that this is all there is.

What themes are emerging as you catch your thoughts, feelings, and actions?

Pull out your body outline pages from the experiments in chapter three and review your findings. Do you see patterns of response? I would blame others, and look outside myself for my well-being, which makes sense, I was living for others, so others determined how I felt—"good or bad"—so then it would follow that if I did things that pleased them and were "good" and when I felt "bad" it was their fault and they needed to tell me how to fix it!

Find your statement that reflects what you truly believe now for yourself and what you want for yourself in the future. Each moment lays the path to the next moment. Moment-to-moment you create your future.

One morning, I woke from a dream in which I was walking along thinking to myself that I needed to have the exact right thought, say the exact right thing that I wanted, to put positive intentional energy into my body and out into the world and those around me. Each interaction, each step in my dream I was asking myself—do I have the right thinking? Each time I would check I would say yes, this is what I want to be thinking and saying. When I woke I realized that every moment, each small moment was important. Later that morning, in my physical life, I was taking my dog to my car. At the same time my daughter opened the door to leave for school, I had the dog on the leash, my coffee in the same hand and needed to only grab my keys in the opposite direction as the open door. I think very linearly at times and don't like to "back track" so I was going to get my keys, but the dog was pulling to get out the door with my daughter, not once or twice but three times and each time he spilled a bit more of my coffee. I was frustrated and couldn't get my mind off the idea that I needed to grab my keys! I fussed at my daughter and fussed at my dog and fussed at the coffee. Later as I reflected on this moment, I knew that I was not putting the energy I wanted into my body or out into the world. I replayed this scenario. I came up with three alternatives as to how I could have thought, felt and acted in order to create the kind of energy I wanted to have and put out. I realized that I could have gone with the flow and just went out to the car with my daughter, put the dog in my car and my daughter into the car and then went back for my keys. My second scenario could have been that I could have picked a better time to leave. And the last scenario was to have gotten everything ready, keys in hand and perhaps coffee into the car before considering taking the dog with me.

The first rule of improv applies here, and it is to say no matter what is thrown to you "yes, and...." So as in any production, you will stop and reflect on how you really want this scene to play out, what is your true motivation, what do you really feel and think. So do a "take two." Stop the scene because you are the producer, director, and actor of your life. Take charge! You are more in control than you might believe.

Think of a situation that didn't turn out like you would have liked, or one in which it left you feeling that you could have done it better. As you replay the situation, come up with at least three different ways that you would have rather had the situation play out and to put only the energy you want to feel and to put out into the world. Imagine each new perspective in your mind and change history. You will have found the corrected scenario when you have shifted the energy to what you wanted to feel.

Situation

_____

_____

Perspective change #1:

_____

_____

Perspective change #2:

_____

_____

Perspective change #3:

_____

_____

MOVING ON

You are ready to move on to the next chapter when you have completed all the experiments from this chapter. You will have started to experiment with ways that you can create space, broken a pattern and made a new pattern and noticed how making these changes felt in your body, and you will have reimagined at least one situation from three different perspectives.

CHAPTER EIGHT:

THOUGHTS REFLECT OUR BELIEFS

ELIEFS ABOUT MYSELF RAN DEEP AND LONG—BUT WERE they mine, or a result of where I was and who I was around? Maybe my beliefs about myself started forming when the nurse held me as an infant, just inside the hospital room door where my birth mother was recovering from her delivery. I often visualize that moment, my birth mother, alone, no family or friends beside her, no congratulations, flowers or cards, no celebration of a birth and the efforts on her part. Was she wondering what she would do next in her life? Adults finalizing the decision to put me up for adoption, her signing papers to confirm her wishes. I wondered about how she rationalized the decision, why she felt it was the best thing for her and me. I wondered if she felt shame for having gotten pregnant, anger at the man who raped her, anger at her mother for being harsh and judging her and sending her away. I imagine the grief she must have felt for her dad who had died a year before. I understood and understand that the undoing of this time together was the only way forward for my birth mom. Undo, undo, undo this dreadful wrong.

After I came out as gay, my parents shut off communication and I decided that I wanted to know what other family I had in the world. I had my adoption records and knew the name of the agency my parents had gone through to get me. I contacted them and though my case was closed, they gave me pointers on how to locate my birth family. I did the research and put two and two together. I composed a letter that I sent to my birth mother's mother, my grandmother. I asked her to make the decision to forward the letter to my birth mom if she felt that it was right. She did, and I received a letter back from my birth mother. Eventually I flew out to meet her and the rest of my family. I was 36-years old. She told me she thought of me often and always loved me.

My birth mother told me that the nurse stood there holding me at her hospital room door and said, "Look what you've done." She lay there, vulnerable, wounded in body, heart and soul, with all of these thoughts and emotions, as a stranger holding her child shamed her for the consequence of being a woman, for bringing life into this world, for bearing the result of selfishness, carelessness, instant need, desire and gratification.

The result was my life.

The fact that my birth mother remembered this statement 36 years later tells me that the energy of it was lasting, that her belief in this statement and all the thoughts and emotions that went with it resonated with her deeply. It was a loaded statement. "Look what you've done." It was filled with implied sexism, victimhood, patriarchal standards, and religious judgement. And perhaps all of this was energetically passed along to me. As the result of all of these beliefs it was now all laid onto me. I now carried the energy of shame, heartache, hurt, anger, loss, wrongness, and loneliness.

The awareness of my belief about myself only compounded throughout my childhood. In my child's mind I made bottom-line black-and-white statements based on these internal feelings, which in turn resulted in more of the same. My world then reflected these back to me. If I believed that I was not valuable, others dismissed me also in various ways, ignoring my thoughts and feelings, leaving me alone, making decisions for me, showing me how I could please them. The end result was that I could not trust myself.

When I did what others told me to do, I was supported, praised and happy feelings were felt all around. This only reinforced that I alone was not enough. And it put into motion the reality that others were responsible for my happiness and my sadness, I was a victim. As I went off to college and into my adult life, I was unprepared to manage life confidently. The conflict became more apparent when I allowed people who I didn't even know to dictate my inner emotional wellbeing and I searched how to please them. I trusted people too easily and searched for instant connections when in reality none were there. I assumed they had my best interests at heart and that they knew better than me about me. When I started to tune into my thoughts I heard a critical voice, corrective, and that voice filled me with doubts. My mind would add past failures to support the argument that I was not enough. I continued to look outside of myself for the answers, the "right" next step, to achieve the right job, the right relationships, all in search of capturing that same feeling that others were pleased with me.

At the time I did not understand the energy behind the beginnings of my life but I knew I wanted to change history. I instinctively knew that even though the outcome would be the same, that I would be adopted, I wanted to change the feelings created that day. I wanted to be loved, to feel celebrated. For my birth mother to feel love, to feel a great sense of accomplishment at creating and giving me my life and to feel hopeful for her life.

I drew a picture in black-and-pink charcoal. And in this picture, instead of the nurse holding me, my birth mother was holding me, swaddled in a soft pink blanket made just for me. We melted into each other, feeling safe, secure, and we felt love. The energetic result was a sense of completion, connection and value in both of our lives. The two beginning developmental attachment stages are called fog and symbiosis, they would have been quick, fleeting even, but enough to have started life with. (We'll learn more about these stages later in the chapter). Of course, others, perhaps the foster care mother who took care of me for a few months could have provided this to me, my adopted mother and father also stepped in and filled in these gaps. And it would have been easier for all of them and me had this process been started moments and days after my birth with the only life I had known for the past nine months.

We all go through variations of birth trauma because we are going from one environment to another. I had spent my life trying to change the environment in order to fill in the gaps, to get it "right." As I studied about reactive attachment disorder and the developmental stages of attachment, I began to see how epigenetic research explains responses to our early environments. As early as six months in the womb our bodies begin to make genes in response to that environment. If my birth mother was sad, angry, shamed, alone and depressed then, the chemicals in her body were also coursing through mine. Once I was born, I moved into the first stage of attachment which is called the "fog stage" and instinctively searched for the one person I had known all my life to feel if my world was secure. Indeed at this stage there is no sense of other or self and safety is directly attached to the mother and her own sense of well-being. When that one person was not around, gaps began to occur. Sense-making of the environment I landed into became more complicated. Learning that I was safe, that I would be taken care of in turn, that this world was safe and that it would take care of me was the only focus. I imagined that perhaps a hypervigilance and a sensitivity was set into motion as a survival skill at this moment.

Once I got married I believed that I had finally done everything right. In this right decision I discovered a freedom I had not felt before. Constrictions that had been placed on me by my mother gradually lifted and I slowly realized a weight was no longer there. I no longer had to be available whenever she called, she no longer checked on my every move, thought and emotion. I no longer felt judged, criticized and wrong. I no longer felt the strong urge to please her and reach for positive responses from her.

I was finally left alone by my mother's critical eye, released from her doubts about me, worry about me, my future, my choices. She had let go energetically to her sense of responsibility to me once I was married.

I didn't realize it as it was happening, I couldn't have articulated it, but I slowly began to feel the difference over time. Instead, we stepped into the role of friends. My stomachaches started to go away. And, though I still had anxiety, my thoughts were allowed to evolve. I heard other voices besides my mother's.

I started to recognize my *own* voice, my *own* thoughts and to look at how these past thoughts did not fit with what I was now believing about myself. I was valuable, worthy, my voice was heard and validated. Others supported my voice, they listened and heard me—the women in my group at church, other mothers, my children. My confidence grew as I realized that I was smart, funny, knowledgeable and I had even learned some things.

With new beliefs intact, my inner world was being reflected back from the outer world. I wasn't being picked apart. I wasn't being judged. My words weren't being ignored or questioned. I began to have experiences of being believed, trusted. All of these thoughts from others reflected back to me, and even though they felt different they definitely felt better. I pulled from my dad's qualities of wisdom, patience, calm, his acceptance of everything and everyone. The contrast of feeling good and then still not-so-good was getting clearer and clearer. When I experienced anxiety and depression it was even more incongruent and uncomfortable. I still had one foot on the gas pedal and one on the brake but my tank was slowly getting filled with new fuel, healthy fuel but there was a bit of gunk left.

Doubts would creep in. I still was sensitive to reflections of myself that I interpreted as negative. I was hyper-vigilant looking for flaws within myself and in the world outside of myself. And I still had beliefs that I wasn't enough. As I reflected on what I attracted into my life, as I went out into the world, the perspective of the perfect "front" without guidance of how to manage or resolve all of the things I was feeling, hurt feelings, or disagreements, kept me looking for things outside of myself. If it looked "good" then it must be right and I needed to have that too. I see now that these thoughts attracted people who also thought this way. This perspective embodied in myself and others reflected a mindset of "what's in it for me?" or "does this benefit me?" kind of questioning. This set up a loop of using others to that end and being used for their own end whether it was for status, the look, popularity, whatever gain seemed most important at the time.

This is betrayal energy, being taken advantage of, and it is also relying solely on others for "success." What was painful time and again, was that these types of others were unreliable at best and trust could not be built. Beliefs run deep and long. As I raised my children, I saw this even more, how could I put this burden on them? I also began to see how I created their world, how what I did and what I said affected them. I found myself re-parenting myself as I parented them. I gave them lots of physical affection, cuddles and kisses. I would break things down and explain situations, talk them through transitions to ease any fears. I would name the feelings they were acting out and we would talk about why they might be feeling this way. I gave them choices and helped them develop their own understanding of what they liked and didn't like. I picked my battles and would only "go to war" with them about things surrounding safety and respect. I used my highly honed skill of adaptability to allow them to be their own unique humans. And in doing all this for them, I allowed myself these privileges as well. Still, my unease grew, as my past thoughts that perpetuated my beliefs were shifting and I had yet to totally dismantle those beliefs that weren't serving me.

Most of my life I identified my worth based on what I did, where I worked, how much I made, titles and accomplishments and how I looked. I was a human doing, not a human being. Now that I was only a stay-at-home mom, my life seemed to be on hold, still living for someone else. I poured my *doings* into painting, decorating the home and church activities but that wasn't important to me, well, not enough. Others in my women's group felt the same. Women were supposed to do it all, full time jobs, raising children, running the house—keeping it clean, cooking the dinner and keeping our husbands happy. I reminded my women's group as well as myself that just because we were not working didn't mean we weren't doing something important—this this was our mission. I wondered why some women could feel so confident and worthy, happy, and content in their roles when I always felt so pushed to do more, do better, chasing a moving goal post. Subtle and not-so-subtle messages around not getting enough money from my husband fed into my feelings of unworthiness. As I watched my husband's affection for our daughter, I felt my own lack and need for attention in order to feel good about myself. I felt the old feeling from when I was growing up where I was invisible, running in the background trying to do everything right in order to please, to be seen, to receive affection and love. My depression emerged again, and I felt hopeless, trapped.

Normally this is when I would leave. Leave the job, the relationship, the city. I would change my environment to try and fill in the gaps, create hope and get it "right" the next time. But now, instead, I looked within and slowly realized that this lack was within me and was a result of how I viewed the world and who I was in it.

On my walks I learned not to look frantically for the answers, but to stop my mind, accept the silence and be still, to receive. If I was truly worthy and valuable then the glimpses into a new world would reflect this power. I began to look at my beliefs and I turned the focus to see that I had believed I was a failure, that I wasn't good enough, didn't have anything of value to say, that my thoughts and feelings didn't matter.

I also realized that I was more in control than I knew. As I dismantled my beliefs and the thoughts that fed them, I realized this wasn't what I really believed or wanted to believe at all. I wanted to apply what others seem to believe about themselves—an acceptance of who they were. I realized that others who believed I was valuable also believed that *they* were valuable.

And I realized that if I held onto my old beliefs they would keep playing out the old loop of coping strategies of blaming others. But if I started to believe in *myself* and take responsibility for who I was, I began to trust that every moment I could create the next moment and my future self.

Part of this was to accept myself as gay. If I dismissed and ignored this knowing, I rejected this part of myself. Beliefs that were emerging were that I was valuable, I was supposed to be alive, I had a place here on this Earth, I had purpose, I was loved authentically for who I was and who I was learning I truly was. This love was more powerful than anything I had ever felt. I realized that I could not adapt my beliefs for people who only loved me if I acted a certain way or lived a certain way. I realized that it was not my job to live my life to make others feel more comfortable. I realized that I alone would be living with my decision, and I would only be prolonging the incongruence within me if I did not accept it.

Sure, there would be a burst of excitement as we embarked on a new situation, and just like all the changes I had made throughout my life to find that elusive missing something, it would fade. And I would be left, again with anxiety, knowing I was living a lie, depression, longing and regrets, looking for the next thing, the next change to distract me, to create the illusion that all was fine. I would be back in situations, trying to manage my thoughts and emotions based on beliefs that didn't reflect my life. I would be left to manage the result of this incongruence alone. I would slowly die inside by the compromises I would make. I would no longer be able to trust myself and what I knew to be true. If I did not act on this, how could I be my best human to serve others?

Beliefs run deep and long—my birth mom eventually moved to my city and spent more time with me and my family.

More of her family moved to my city. I met aunts and uncles and cousins and their children. We spent holidays and celebrations together. I learned I had a younger half-brother, who was not given up for adoption but raised by my mom and her husband and his children. Over time, I still didn't feel a strong connection to her. I saw the dysfunction and felt burdened in her presence and with the entire family. The burden I felt around her soon revealed itself as she voiced that she too struggled with me being gay. She started to demand that I spend more and more time with her, alone, without my partner, and even though I had attempted to undo the negative energy of my birth day, I began to feel that she too placed blame on me, needing me to fix her by being "right" for her.

I was still not enough in her eyes. One day she told me that my communication and visits with her were not enough. And because of this it felt like a dagger in her heart that was being twisted each time we would interact. I realized then, that I was once again hurting her. I was being blamed for her pain, her wounding, that she still believed the nurse's statement, that her mistakes defined who she was. Her beliefs had not changed, even though I was working hard at changing mine.

In the beginning, as I wrestled with what to do with my newfound information about my sexual identity, I tried on a variety of scenarios. One which would tick the boxes off, the one my husband and my parents wanted, was to stay married. We contacted a realtor to sell our house and move to Colorado. I could go to seminary there and my husband could transfer with the same company. We even had family close by and my parents could visit more often. Others in our church community shared that they had seen these types of friendships grow with other women in the past and they too had moved away from the relationships to keep their marriages and families intact. We were supported in this move and the pieces were falling into place easily. We would move away from my friend and start over. So, we told my parents the good news and within hours I received the biggest bouquet of flowers from my mom that I had ever seen.

It hit me in the moment as I held the flowers the delivery person gave me, that as I received them, I was accepting old patterns of living my life for someone else's comfort. I was again looking outside of myself for approval, validation and acceptance. I sat down right there on the hallway floor and looked inside. I listened as I heard words of my truth. I listened to the small voice, now getting louder. I listened to my intuition and I knew that I would be back to this place again, it was not going away. Being gay was not a learned behavior, a fad, or whim, it was genetic. Epigenists acknowledge that 2% of the genes that we are born with are hard-wired, like our skin, hair and eye color and defects that might occur. And that the X and Y chromosomes that determine gender are much more fluid than previously known, believed or observed, which results in a variety of combinations of Xs and Ys.

I was finding my voice. I was experiencing being listened to, heard and believed. I was learning as I listened to my thoughts and allowed myself to feel my emotions. I saw my outward actions, that anxiety and depression, blaming others and shutting down, were not how I wanted to live my life. I stopped putting "my" in front of thoughts, emotions and actions and realized they weren't mine at all. They were not what I would choose. The thoughts I kept hearing in my head were my interpretations from my child brain, messages that I heard and observed. In my childlike, black-and-white thinking said, "I'm not good enough." If I believed that "I was good enough" then my coping strategies no longer fit. My thoughts that supported were new. I was experiencing new emotions besides anxiety and depression, I was feeling hopeful. My beliefs about myself were changing. People pleasers can apply the reverse Golden Rule: Treat yourself as you would treat others.

One day after a therapy session, I noticed a sign on a storefront advertising for Aura Photography. Acting on my inner voice these days, I quickly turned my car into the parking lot. Aura photography tapped into my growing understanding of chakras, and I knew that some people could see this energy. I was intrigued how a camera could pick this up. I learned that by charging an object with electricity while it sits on a photographic plate, you can create a colorful and distinctive image of the discharge as it comes off the body.

I walked out of the session with a photo image of purple light surrounding my entire body. I learned that purple meant Intuitive, playful, visionary, nonjudgmental, unconventional, and inspired. I also learned that it meant that I should avoid feeling overwhelmed, and that I must trust my vision and share it with others. And, oh, keep a journal.

I believe that everyone is born worthy and that our worth is intertwined with our very being. Our concept of our own self-worth is reinforced by our actions. Each time we take the time to appreciate ourselves, treat ourselves kindly, define personal boundaries, be proactive in having our needs met, and allow other perspectives, we express our recognition of our innate value. I believe that love is everywhere. I believe that the world is safe and will meet our needs. I believe we are more than our experiences and our body's responses to them.

I believe that there are lessons to be learned in each moment. I believe that support is always there if we turn our gaze to receive it. I believe that God is spirit and spirit is energy and Energy makes up everything in the Universe and is accessible to everyone. In fact, I believe that we are swimming in Energy. It reminds me of a cartoon drawing I once saw that shows two fish swimming in water and one says, "You know, I don't know if I believe in water." I believe that once we begin to understand the ways of the energy of the universe we will open up to endless possibilities. I believe it begins with each individual and is manifested out into the world. I believe, as so many others have said in various ways, "If you change your beliefs, you change your world."

To know what you believe, look at your thoughts. Which is what I have encouraged you to do throughout this book.

SUMMARY

This chapter discussed the subject of beliefs and using our thoughts to uncover hidden beliefs that may no longer serve us. In the experiments below you will learn more about how to uncover your hidden beliefs that are sabotaging your efforts, and you will be guided to begin to formulate new beliefs that will carry you forward into creating the life you truly want.

EXPERIMENT #15:

IDENTIFY FOUNDATIONAL GAPS

Below is a description of the developmental stages of attachment that we all go through. We don't just go through them when we are first born, though this is the first round, we repeat these stages with all our relationships and with ourselves.

129

DEVELOPMENTAL STAGES OF ATTACHMENT

1. FOG (THE FIRST FEW DAYS, WEEKS AND MONTHS OF LIFE)

The caregiver and infant are in a fog, meaning they are learning about each other. In this stage, the trust cycle occurs and also the first step of attachment—which is TRUST. The caregiver and the infant are just getting to know each other. This is where the infant's needs are met again and again. The infant will cry, the caregiver will comfort them, change them, feed them and there will be a sigh of contentment and relaxation. And this is done over and over, enough that the infant believes that his world is safe and they can trust it to take care of them.

2. SYMBIOSIS (FROM FOUR-TO SIX-WEEKS OLD TO FIVE-MONTHS OLD)

This stage is characterized by feelings of falling in love. The symbiotic gaze is in this stage and it is also the second step of attachment which is positive interaction. There is an exchange of glances, smiles and laughter, which feels like a connection between the infant and caregiver.

3. DIFFERENTIATION (FROM FIVE-MONTHS OLD TO NINE-TO 10-MONTHS OLD)

The infant begins to turn outward and discover that self and caregiver are different. "Checking in" is an important sign of the child's connection to the caregiver. Just like adults call their mates from work, the toddler looks to the caregiver for reassurance. Checking is discovering the difference between caregiver and not caregiver.

4. Practicing (from nine-to-ten-months old to 15-to-16-months old)

The infant is getting the feel of being apart and of feeling safely connected at this stage. Crawling occurs in the beginning of the practicing stage and represents the baby's ability to move away from the warmth of the caregiver's presence. Refueling—babies can maintain their sense of connectedness by holding the caregiver's safety with an object called transitional objects. Slowly the child begins to be able to discard the object as permanence and constancy are internalized and they feel safe and whole in varying situations.

5. Rapprochement (15-to-28 months old)

This is the UH OH, we really are two separate people AND I want the safety of symbiosis. In this stage there is a return of dependent behaviors and anxiety at separation. The toddler is overwhelmed by the dawning reality that they exist separately and that outweighs their beginning capacity to know that caregivers exist even when they can't see, hear, or touch them. So the toddler will woo the caregiver back into that symbiotic-connection stage. When the toddler is able to get the caregiver to focus on them he feels safe again and he is refueled to try again. If the wooing fails, the toddler becomes coercive and may hit, kick, throw temper tantrums etc. as a last-ditch attempt to avoid the anxiety of being separate. Many relationships break down at this stage. The constancy from attached relationships is that they experience each other as whole and stable whose nurturance is available even when there is tension. That is the glue that holds the relationship together. And that is when the child has reached the last stage.

6. Consolidation of Individuation (36-54 months)

Two whole people joined by trust, positive interactions, and a sense of belonging sustained by the capacity to hold the existence and the constancy of the other. This is the beginning of the child's individuality. The child learns that the caregiver is still the caregiver whether they are tired, energetic, happy, or sad and if that is the same caregiver that nurtures then their nurturing is available, if not now, then soon. The child can safely function as a separate person most of the time.

As you look over these stages, think back to your beginnings and reflect on where you struggle today. Reflect on the questions below and write your thoughts down.

- Do you lack trust with others? or do you trust too easily? (Fog)
- Do you rush too fast into falling in love, before you trust? Or do you struggle to make connection with others? (Symbiosis)
- Do you view differences as wrong, or bad? Do you push others away or keep them too close? (Differentiation)
- Are you comfortable doing things alone or do you always need someone with you? (Practicing)
- Do you push others away, or do you feel insecure when you are by yourself? (Reproachment)
- Do you feel unprepared or incapable of taking care of yourself? Or do you do everything all by yourself not needing anyone's help or support? (Consolidation of Individuation)

These questions reflect the extremes of each stage, and you might find these to be true for yourself at times or you may feel you are somewhere in between. Likely your current behaviors will point back to moments in time when you were wounded or there are gaps in one or more of these stages of attachment.

Notes:

_____

_____

_____

_____

_____

_____

EXPERIMENT #15

IDENTIFY CURRENT BELIEFS

Think about the messages you received and learned as you grew up and how your child's mind interpreted them with black-and-white types of statements. For example mine were, "Everyone hates me," "I'm stubborn", "My feelings don't matter," "I don't have anything to offer." And maybe some more positive ones, "I'm a good artist, singer, dancer, musician, writer" Ahh, do you see that my negative ones are character flaws, and my positive ones are roles? Maybe you will discover these themes for yourself as well. Reflect on the questions below:

What do others reflect onto me that might create my inner thoughts?

_____

_____

_____

What do others believe you to be?

_____

_____

_____

What are your current beliefs?

_____

_____

_____

Do these beliefs reflect your inner thoughts and emotions?

_____

_____

_____

EXPERIMENT #16

IDENTIFY YOUR NEW BELIEF

What would you *rather* be thinking and feeling? Look back in Chapter Six at **Experiment #9: Challenge the negative messages and Experiment #10: Replace negative thoughts.** As you reflect on your negative messages consider the questions below.

What thoughts support old beliefs and the messages that came with them?

_____

_____

Align your challenged messages (Experiment #9) and replacement thought (Experiment #10) to create a new belief statement. For example, if you are thinking "I have accomplished___", "I have completed ___", "I am proud that I ____" what belief supports this way of thinking? If you have accomplished something you may say that you are valuable, you are worthy.

_____

_____

Do your new thoughts support your new beliefs?

_____

_____

My new belief about myself is:

_____

_____

EXPERIMENT #17

PRACTICE

Run your new belief through everything you think and feel and do. Moment-to-moment, catch your thoughts and emotions and realign them with your new belief in yourself. Write your new belief down, make a poster, put it on a post-it note, put the post it notes everywhere. Say it to yourself and check your thoughts moment-to-moment. Are your thoughts supporting your new beliefs in yourself? If not, replay the situation, reimagine another way to have said or done it until it supports your belief and make it so.

As you go through this experiment carve out time at the end of your day to reflect on situations or conversations that happened throughout your day.

Did you say, do, think, and feel in ways that support your new Belief?

_____

_____

Did your new belief support you—did it help you manage through to getting it right?

_____

_____

MOVING ON:

You are ready to move onto the next chapter when you have completed the experiments in this chapter. Did you identify a development stage of attachment that needs to be addressed? And have you discovered that your negative messages are connected to this gap? Have you noticed that the negative messages support an old belief? Were you able to identify what you would rather be thinking and feeling and from there create a new belief?

CHAPTER NINE:

LETTING GO

THE PARADOX OF LETTING GO IS THAT IT FEELS WHEN WE DO it as though we will be losing something in the process. We are. It might be a friend, a parent, a job, a way of life, a belief, a perception. And yet if we don't let go we cannot hold on to the next thing.

In the process of intentionally letting go of something that no longer fully supports intentional living, we learn that we aren't losing something but gaining exactly what we want and need to continue to grow. Imagine a dog with a stick in his mouth chasing after a ball you just threw. He is now in a dilemma. The dog (like you in any scenario) has free will, a choice. Does he drop the stick in order to get the ball, try to put both in his mouth, leave one and run around and go back to the other, back-and-forth or maybe neither—it's too confusing so the dog might settle for neither the stick or the ball. Until the dog makes a choice either one is an option and so too, inaction is an active choice. To not make a choice, essentially choosing inaction, you are saying that neither the ball or the stick is right for you.

You could think of this process of letting go in this way—making a choice. Trying to have both will create chaos and confusion. Choosing one might mean you chose the wrong one, while waiting for the next option, may leave you with nothing. Up until now you have been narrowing down how to make this choice for yourself. You have been asking "Which is better for me, the stick or the ball?" You have been asking what you truly believe about yourself. "Does this thought support my beliefs?" "Does this way of perceiving the situation support my beliefs?" or "Do I need to try something else?"

When I came out as gay, many of the people around me were confused at best. Some were angry, others sad or disappointed. Not only was I changing my beliefs and perceptions and rocking my own world, but I was also challenging the beliefs and perceptions that others held of me and themselves too. One action sets into motion other actions and we are all connected in this way. At the time, I felt a sense that I can only describe as a universal urgency. It was bigger than myself, more powerful than myself. There was a push so hard, so loud and uncomfortable that I could not ignore it. I felt the magnitude and the weight. I felt the energy of this but did not fully understand that by coming out I would shift the energy of not only my world, but *the* world, the universe, in a way that would put a multitude of events into motion.

I did have a choice, but by now, I felt very guided, corralled, and supported to make the choice that would alter my life. From there, the sorting process began. For those that took my coming out as an opportunity to glance into their own beliefs and see that I had a place there, they became supportive and reflected back value and love. Those that either chose not to examine their beliefs or challenge them enough to find a place for me, did not stick around. Each of their choices provided me with information about those people and who they were and how they fit into my life. These choices allowed me the opportunity to be in the process of letting go. I am still in this process as I continue to replay and hear more clearly the choices that others make in response to my life. I let them go. I allow them to live their life and to learn and grow the way that they will choose.

You are the curator of your life.

Your life is your story alone and you and only you are in charge of writing it. As writer and psychoanalist Clarissa Pinkola- Estés says in her wonderful storytelling ways, "You are the one, the only, the best." Instead of despair, choose hope. Instead of cynicism, choose hope. Instead of doubt, choose hope. And always choose love. You are the director, producer and actor of your life. You alone decide the plot, the motivation, and the purpose of your character. This is not TikTok but a long-running Netflix series with depth and intention, twists and turns, intrigue and excitement that only free will can provide.

When we check our beliefs, our thoughts and our perceptions, we are in a better position to rearrange the rest of our lives. We keep learning as we peel back the many facets of our beliefs/perceptions. The real fact is that you are never done because we live in a world that is constantly changing. And if we get into that flow of change and get out of the way, it doesn't feel like change, it feels—exactly right. Like water flowing down a river not hitting the rocky sides of the banks.

Or you could think of it like a room filled with boxes. The big boxes, the obvious ones, are right in front of you demanding your attention. And as you haul them away, and let them go, you see the next row of boxes and the next until you get to the back of the room where it is dark, no one has been there for a long time, if ever. You get out a flashlight and shine into the corners and crevices and begin to clean out there as well. Don't keep the boxes and the gunk, throw it away, transform it, recycle it in your garden, put it in a compost, allow it to get in the flow of life, to decay, and transform into new growth. This is your work with beliefs and perceptions, ideals that are no longer working for you need to be let go. If we clear away only the boxes and leave the gunk in the corners and crevices we will be back again to clean up as the gunk spreads to the new boxes. Your new beliefs will have the residue of the old on them, like a fast-growing mold.

You now know your themes, your beliefs, and the various ways they show up in your life, you know what you are looking for, you can recognize it, and name it. Your mind is clever, and you see how quickly, even in the concentrated effort, to think differently, it will loop back to an old pattern, but now less and less. In times of stress, you watch as your mind reverts to its old familiar ways but does not stay there as long. Your old beliefs have put you in an invisible prison and you are learning the key to breaking free each time you challenge old beliefs and step into your new ones.

When we first moved into my parents' house I smelled mold and had for years when I would visit. Dad would say, oh it's just the basement, it's the water damage from leaking when it rains. I had taken a fake plant to my work that had been sitting on the stairwell down to the basement. Soon the office and down the hallways began to smell. My colleagues and the cleaning staff started to try to identify where this odor was coming from and much to my shame they carted my plant out to the garbage. The smell of the mold had traveled all the way to my workplace. Like beliefs and perceptions, I was not so aware of the smell because I lived in the house, it had become my normal and like my dad had thought, well it's just a wet basement smell. When others smelled it though, they responded, they acted, they pointed it out and they helped me see there was a problem. They helped me to know that I alone had to get rid of the mold and act. I had the air and the mold checked later when I moved back into that same home, and discovered that there were level-three mold spores growing in the basement and permeating through the air in the entire house. I hired a company with expertise in cleaning up this kind of thing. They sealed off the basement and in their hazmat suits. Wearing goggles and gloves, they stripped the basement, they threw out old blankets, trunks, dolls, wooden chairs, doors, work benches, bricks, wood beams, acoustic sealing, walls and screens. I had the air ducts cleaned that spread the mold spores to the second floor. I had sub pumps installed to pump the water out at a constant rate from the water table below the house. I had the walls and windows sealed, fixed the plumbing and scrubbed the floors. The new boxes and items that I now place in the basement do not—and will not—get mold on them.

When I moved back to my hometown to be near my dad as he moved into a retirement home, several things had to shift in order for this to occur or even be considered. Prior to this time, my mom had been in a 20-year decline with Alzheimer's disease. I had only learned of my mom's state two years prior when I was invited to visit. It was during this trip that I told mom that my wife and I were expecting our child. We had been looking at old pictures of my younger self and my older kids and reminiscing, mom encouraging me to take things from the house that she showed me. I asked her if she thought that dad would like to know about our baby and she said no, her disappointment again in her voice at my life choices. She reflected how hard I made life for everyone. At this point, I was both hopeful and sad knowing that within 20 minutes she would have forgotten our conversation. As I left from that trip I asked my parents if we could talk more frequently on a regular basis, maybe even by phone, and after some thought, they informed me that they were good with the way it was, meaning no contact unless they contacted me. I was again put in a position of waiting, longing, hopefulness that maybe one day they would accept me for who I am. My response was to send my mom cards with lighthearted notes inside. Three years later when I moved back to my family house, displayed on the counter were two of the cards I had sent to her that year.

My mom's disease added another layer to the loss of our relationship, and I thought back in my mind knowing that for the better part of my time as being out as gay, she was slowly losing her capacity to remember, to think through things and to evolve in her perspective about me and how she could be in relationship with me. Slowly, a new perspective of realization unfolded as I thought back about the decline in her reaching out to me. Though it was couched in her not feeling comfortable with me, I began to see a bigger picture, more of the truth. I believe that she had been coming around to love me again and accept me, to see that I hadn't changed but that I was living my values, that I embodied integrity that she could admire and stand behind. I remembered how my parents drove for Thanksgiving one year to the home I shared with my then-partner. They sat at our table on the sunny Arizona patio with my kids and our friends.

Less than a year after my last visit home, my mom forgot how to turn and walk properly and she fell. She went into rehab after surgery and then to an Alzheimer's living facility. My dad visited her daily and our line of communication opened tentatively as I found that he answered my emails with details about his life and even responded with inquiries into mine. Within six months my mom got an infection from which she never recovered. She died in October 2017. I could only attend her funeral alone, no wife, no baby, no children, no one to support me. I supported my dad and my dad shielded me from all our relatives whom I had not seen or heard from since I came out in 1995. I didn't realize how much he shielded me until his funeral, when many of these same relatives did not attend. And I realized that they had come to support my dad at my mom's funeral. Those relatives who did attend his funeral found subtle and not-so-subtle ways to reflect their inner thoughts and feelings towards me and my family. I observed and felt their veiled attempts at niceties, their closed body language and outright refusal to answer my smiles and conversation as well as flashes of anger, which I now understand were to defend themselves against a view that I was going to do the same to them! I played my dad's words from the past year over in my head as I sorted through his weighted message to "listen to the silence" from others as their way of communicating to me.

It was not lost on me the silence that he and my mom provided for many years. He was telling me to listen to words that were not said, to listen to actions. I felt another layer of letting go, and the loss that comes with this, as I came to terms with the finality of the loss of these relatives again. One day, I was perceived as a heterosexual married woman with children, an accepted and understood role in the world. I was seemingly financially supported, with abundant resources, with parents, aunts, uncles, cousins, friends in many states where we had lived and moved. The next day all of this was stripped clean away, none of it remained. When we moved back to my hometown, into my parents' house I had naively imagined frequent trips by close relatives to visit, to reclaim a relationship with me that my parents had kept from them. I imagined my brother and my nieces and their families celebrating holidays together, everyone picking out things from the house that they might want, remembering fondly of past times with my parents and building new memories together like when we were kids.

At my dad's funeral though I saw more clearly into their hearts and their beliefs and knew at various levels how they had not only betrayed me but that they had been deceitful even to him. But my dad knew. Once he had moved out of his home, relatives started to try to swoop in and invade what was once his alone. My dad was firm with them and made a point to tell me that he had told them that they were not allowed into his house, now my house, and he would no longer be giving them any more of his money. My dad was once again shielding me. And to this day the shield remains, his silence finally broken.

After my mom's funeral, my dad and I sat watching football enjoying a beer and he, still looking at the last play on the field, said, "How's your baby?" I froze in my seat as the conversation with my mom flashed back into my memory, so many questions that I could not articulate, did mom remember long enough to tell him? Had he overhead? Had my brother betrayed my secret? Bottom line, he knew, and he was asking, and I could be open and honest with him. I began to call him more frequently once I got back home and he knew that we were gearing up to move somewhere else in the world one day. We were actively downsizing and selling our house in preparation. He insisted on staying in his house though we were all concerned, until one day he could no longer stand up. He was rushed to the hospital where they found he had a fracture in his spine. In rehab, he realized that he would never be going back home, and events unfolded rapidly. The day I called my dad, a family friend and her son were there visiting him (unbeknownst to me.) They heard his end of my phone call, in which I tentatively said, "Dad, you know we've been trying to figure out where to move next, what do you think if we would move back home to be with you?" My dad didn't hesitate, and I've never heard him sound happier as he said "Yes! You can live in the house, I'll give you the house, this is the best news I've ever had." Our family friend recalled to me later that after that phone call my dad's demeanor changed so dramatically that they felt his excitement, love and relief all rolled into one. The shifts had already started to create this move and several other details started to fall quickly into place. I watched as my counseling license was easily transferred to this new state, as I was accepted into a new position and my current company allowed me to work remotely. But it was no small feat to move across the country, and it wasn't all easy. My wife had three months left until she finished her bachelor's degree. My daughter needed a preschool so that I could work during the day. And we needed to break our lease that we had just signed for six months, as well as move our cars and purge and pack all our stuff.

One day after my daughter and I completed phase one of our move we were at an unfamiliar Sam's club. My daughter in the cart, I was looking for items, and it was so hard to find them, too much different, too much new, everything was all too much. Seemingly out of the blue, a catch in my throat and tears came to my eyes, a feeling of overwhelming helplessness, lost in the aisles, alone. At the gas pump, the cold wind—whipping my hair aggressively around my face, the screen prompting me to put in a zip code I only remembered when sending my mother cards. I cried. Another change, another perspective, another letting go.

This is not easy work, but I believe it is necessary work.

The definition of insanity is doing the same thing over and over expecting a different result. As scientists, our experiments need intention, they need a purpose, a hypothesis, and they need consistency over a period of time. We need to run the experiment long enough to enable a result, to collect data and make assumptions on the findings. We also need imagination and the capacity to identify what didn't work and to make changes. And we need perseverance— to try again.

SUMMARY:

This chapter addressed the thoughts and emotions that occur during the process of letting go. The experiments below will help you let go of the old by solidifying your new beliefs into something more tangible and it will guide you through to letting go.

EXPERIMENT #18

VISION, MISSION AND VALUES STATEMENT

Think of your life as a corporation—in that you have come into this world to achieve something. You have an idea of what that something is because you now have a belief. From this place, let's get solid with it and define for yourself how you want this belief to reflect out into the world. Every successful corporation has a vision, mission, or value statement. Everything that a corporation does goes through this filter so when opportunities to do this project or that event come along, they look at this statement and decide if it fits. Your beliefs and your perspective of your world are your vision statements, they support the missions you embark upon and the values that you hold.

A mission statement describes the purpose and day-to-day effort. A vision statement describes your ultimate goal or future outcome. The two work in tandem: A vision statement expresses what you ultimately want to achieve. A mission statement articulates what you will do to get there. The overall statement will reflect your new belief.

What do you Value?

_____

_____

Describe your day-to-day efforts and purpose? Or What you would want them to be.

_____

_____

What is your ultimate goal? What do you want your future to look like?

_____

_____

From your thoughts above, create your Vision, Mission and Value Statement.

EXPERIMENT # 19

WRITE YOUR SLOGAN AND YOUR LOGO

Every successful business has a condensed version of the vision, mission and value statements in the form of a slogan. And an image that also reflects their purpose in the form of a logo. We quickly identify what this company stands for. Think about all the major companies and organizations that you know and visualize their logos. Almost immediately you know what they stand for. Look at fast food restaurants, your phone, laptop, amusement parks. Their success is summed up in their slogan and in their logo. You will be representing your new belief through your vision, mission and values statement by creating a shortened version of it into a slogan and logo. Place this logo everywhere, tattoo it on your ankle!

Create your slogan

Create your logo

```

```

EXPERIMENT #20

LET IT GO

When I lived in Arizona we would often drive out to southern California and spend a weekend. This particular weekend four of us were heading home and Sunday afternoon traffic in southern California is intense to say the least. I was driving and my girlfriend was in the front and our couple friends were in the back. As I merged from one freeway to the next freeway my girlfriend was freaking out, she was uncontrollable as she spewed out her concerns and doubts onto me, my driving, my thought process, my competence.

Now, I am a very good driver, I drive defensively. I am tuned into everything around me and go at steady speeds in order to be safe. I will never forget how empowered and supported I felt when I heard my friend from the back seat say, "I think she is doing a great job, and she has this under control." Now that you've tightened up your beliefs and your perspectives of your life, run everything in your life through the filter of this lens. Does it support your vision, your mission and your values? If not, it is not supporting you, and it is taking energy out of you. Don't let the critical front-seat drivers deplete your energy, lean into those that offer support and build you up to be your best, to shine. Let it go, make way for what will support you, what gives you energy and what will help you to grow and be the one, the only, the best.

Letting go of people, places, ideas and things does not mean that they do not have value. You are letting go of your attachment to them and all that they represent.

Sit in a safe, quiet space before you begin this next exercise and visualize or conceptualize what you know you would like to release. Offer this energy to the Earth, so that it can transform it into nutrients to promote new growth. Imagine the energy of what you are letting go. Imagine that it is traveling down through your body out through the soles of your feet. Imagine cool, cleansing water rushing in from the top of your head filling up every part of your inner body and watch as flakes and chunks wash off into the water and flow down and out the soles of your feet, into the Earth. Imagine these flakes and chunks of energy you no longer need or want soaking down into the soil, down into the bedrock, down to the core of the Earth until they are consumed into the heat of the core, they turn to ash and recycle back up to the bedrock, into the soil and grow into something new. Consider that letting go is a natural cycle, necessary to get rid of the old and make way for the new life.

Thoughts to let go of

_____

_____

Feelings to let go of

_____

_____

Things to let go of

_____

_____

Places to let go of

_____

_____

People to let go of

_____

_____

MOVING ON:

You will be ready to move on to the next chapter when you have created vision, mission and values statements that reflect your new belief as well and have made up a slogan and logo to represent them. You will have reflected on what you would like to and need to let go of in order to fully embrace your new belief.

CHAPTER TEN:

WORKING WITH AWARENESS— SPIRIT = ENERGY

N MY 30s, WHEN I FOUND MYSELF ONCE AGAIN DISILLUSIONED with the life I had, I started wondering what the soul was. I read books trying to understand this soul that everyone talked about. How was my soul different from my mind and my thoughts? What's the difference between my soul and spirit and how do I hear it, know it is there?

What is it? How do I access it?

I was so confused and felt I was missing something really important. On my early-morning walks I realized that when my mind was quiet—there was something there. When I focused on writing, drawing, painting or playing music, I got into a zone and at those times I was not just a body, I was more.

I was told I was a sensitive child and would have times when I was crying or angry or frustrated without even knowing why. As a mother, I sat day in and day out with my two small children, meeting their needs and putting mine aside. I grew sadder and sadder, more and more depressed. I loved my children, and I knew I was doing a good job parenting them so why was I so sad? Of course, you know by now that I was looking outside of myself to feel anything and when anybody, warranted or not, takes your energy and it does not get replenished you have nothing left to give. The existential crisis I found myself in created a new desperation to understand what the heck was going on. This can't be all that life is about! What piece was I missing what others seemed to have?

When I was growing up I didn't understand that much of what I was feeling and picking up was coming from outside myself. One day as I was riding in the back of our Ford station wagon I happened to glance out the window to see a boy walking along the street. I told my mom to stop, that our cat was in the trash can this boy had just passed. She didn't stop. And four blocks later we arrived at our house. It was a sunny summer day and I was out of school. It was hot and getting late in the day. I looked desperately around the front yard and the back-yard for my cat. Yelling "Frisky" out into the neighborhood, frantically alone in my quest. The cat was nowhere around the house and without hesitation I jumped on my brand-new purple bike that I just got for my 12th birthday and rode those four blocks back to the very trash can the boy had just passed and there inside was my cat. I was right, no one acknowledged this, no one even seemed to notice. But I had my cat back in her yard and I stayed until the sun set petting her and loving on her. I didn't know what I had tapped into that day as I was being driven down the street in the back of my mom's car. But I remembered this and as my life unfolded I found that I was really feeling the energy of situations, people and things. I learned that the first question to ask when I noticed that I was feeling something or thinking something was, "Is this mine?" As I became more aware, I realized that most always what I felt was not mine. I realized how much I had been living out others' lives, anticipating others' needs, wants, and desires, then waiting for this information to make my next move that it provided a direction. Today I see the importance of thoughts and how we are all affected by them whether they are said aloud or not. I hope throughout this book you have learned this too!

My journey into understanding this unknown, elusive energy started in earnest when I sought to answer the question of how to best help others heal. To that end, it meant finding the common themes that we all experience. When I began studying expressive arts therapy, my world began to open and led to a deeper understanding of how the energy created by the arts can shift our mental and emotional positions. As I stood with others in a studio, floors and walls covered in tarps, we each had a large piece of butcher paper taped to the wall of our own space. I chose paints and brushes and listened to the sounds of music playing in the background. I centered myself and closed my eyes. I began to move my body and my arms to the rhythm of the music. The hand that held my brush found its own unique movement. I chose a paint color and used this same movement onto my butcher paper. As I opened my eyes to look at the image I had created, I again centered myself and gazed at the color and the shapes and asked this movement in form, "What do you need to be fully alive?" I suspended any thoughts to edit or make sense of it, trusting that the image was emerging into something that was supposed to be unknown. I was expectant and excited to see what would emerge as I painted and layered colors, chose ribbons, cloth and buttons, feathers, beads and bobbles. After hours in the zone of creativity, I was exhilarated, exhausted and excited to see what came out. I sat in front of a figure of a dancing woman that I had never met before and asked her questions:

"What is your name?" "Why are you here?" "What do you have to tell me?" From the answers I received, I became aware of a new perspective and a new way of expressing what I wasn't even aware was inside me.

In my expressive arts coursework, we would often start our time together in music. We would stand in a circle together, calling one another into the circle. Each person one-by-one would sing their name and everyone would sing it back to them in the same tone, pitch, and strength. We would sing long, drawn-out *As Es Is Os* and *Us*, toning together and hearing the harmony of different voices melding together increasing in sound and strength and volume and then sliding away as each of us slowly in our time lost our breath. When we gathered for drum circles, everyone would pick out their own percussion instrument: a drum, cymbals, wooden flute, shaker, wood blocks, claves, cowbells, chimes and then we would explore the sound that the instrument makes. The result is a cacophony of tones and beats. With the mother drum—the biggest, deepest-sounding drum in the circle—a steady beat began to pull us all together. As others continued to explore their instrument they found their rhythm, their song, and soon we all would hear the sounds around us. We found our place in the gaps and put our own rhythms and sounds into them. After 20 minutes or less the entire circle reached an understanding, and as a collective potential and we hit those sweet "Ah Ha" moments of connecting. Faces would vibrate and beam around the circle of concentration and recognition of this moment and we would all try even harder to recreate the connection. In this musical vibration, I found a new way of connecting with others and a new way of feeling validated. The vibration of music shifted my inner body and my awareness of my emotional body increased. I listened and felt heard.

Energy/spirit was at work during these times and I learned that the vibration of music can shift the energy in our bodies. A high tone can decrease the pressure of a sinus headache. Alpha waves, delta waves and theta waves can create the brain waves to entrain with our neurons, putting us into an alert state, a meditative state, or a learning state. Musical notes vibrate at different frequencies which create their unique sound, and these frequencies create different colors. Some people even see music in color as they tune into the vibration. This is why we can put a color to chakras and auras. Everything is vibrating. Finding time in your day for music can shift your vibration.

Everything is vibrating because everything is energy. We can consider the vibration of thoughts and feelings as well. We even have language that reflects this when we say, "I feel down," "I'm high as a kite," "I'm not feeling connected," " I don't have the energy for this." We even know that feeling down can be an energy drain on us and it pulls down the energy of everyone around us. We know that when we are feeling good, others feel good too and want to be around us. All energy goes out into the world. We feel the energy of our emotions and thoughts of those around us, whether we realize it or not. This chapter is about acknowledging that this is happening.

Imagine a time when you may have walked into a room after others had been arguing. You can feel the tension, this is not yours, but you are feeling it. When you meet someone and you can't quite define why, but you just don't like them or maybe you *do* like them and can't really explain why. You might be responding to the vibration they are putting out into the world.

We have two cats and two dogs in our house and there is one cat that the dogs and the other cat just don't like. He is always chased or howled at. The pets just aren't vibing with him. And as humans we all vibrate at different wavelengths.

Those that are vibrating closest to our vibration are the ones we will connect with. Those that are not, we don't connect with. It's not good or bad, it just is. These are the laws of the universe. Imagine the dimples on a golf ball, choose a dimple and you can see that if that represented you and all the other dimples represented everyone else in the world that your perspective would be very different from the dimple on the other side of the ball. The perspective of those dimples closer to you would be more similar to yours. Another law of physics applies here in that two objects can not occupy the same space at the same time. We all have our place, and one person's place does not negate your place or theirs. Give weight to this knowledge as you navigate and continue to grow your awareness. You are not wrong in what you are feeling.

As I continued my energy exploration by growing the gap between my thoughts in meditation, stretching and releasing the body in yoga poses and asanas, running, movement of all kinds, all of these activities were building my body awareness and integrating my body with the mind. Throughout this book you have become more and more aware of your body and the messages it is reflecting to you. You are in a human body and experience all of what it is able to experience, and you are learning more about your body and how to manage this body and allow it to do what you want.

As I studied the interplay of our chakras and meridians, my world opened to the earth elements of Traditional Chinese Medicine, and how stones, scents, herbs, and times of day all affect our body and consequently our emotional states. One day I booked an appointment for a past-life regression, which opened the door to understanding and experiencing my existence as fluid and timeless. In the session I remember visiting several lives in my past, each time prompted to look down at the shoes I was wearing. In many of my lives I was male, and I felt this explained how I was so easily in touch with both my masculine and feminine identities. In one life I looked down and saw shoes like those worn in Mongolia, turned up at the toe.

I studied the I Ching learning about times of change, Buddhism learning Reincarnation, Karma, Meditation, The Four Noble Truths, Noble Eightfold Path, and The Five Precepts. I looked to Native Americans regarding their connection to nature. As I ran my new understanding through my upbringing in the Christian church it revealed how for millennia, societies have been creating ritual around change, curiosity of the larger work at play and an unknown force affecting us, as well as sense of gratitude and a humility to just be alive. I studied the metaphors of the body and its messages. And I studied quantum theory, epigenetics, and behavioral science. I saw the interplay of our behaviors and knew that all of it had the ability to be transformed into whatever we wanted. We are more powerful than we know or are able to grasp. At the same time, we are so small in comparison to what is outside of ourselves. In my mind I wove the common threads that all these theories and techniques, philosophies and beliefs and were attempting to achieve. And I realized that harnessing energy within us and from all around us was the key to gaining optimal health. I was not asking new questions when I explored this energy work and my eyes were opened to the nuances of the world we live in.

When I began studying energy healing through IQM, how to work with my energy knowledge took place. The pieces fell together and tapped into the vastness as well as the smallest nuances of what makes up all of the universe. My dictionary had the missing pieces filled in and at every level of existence

I began to see how we can continue to take out the old boxes of our psyches. As IQM practitioners we often say we are garbage collectors, the merry maids of cleaning up energy—that's all. And as you strengthen your trust in yourself and your path, you too will want to know more, and you too can learn how to do this for yourself. To clean up after yourself.

We all have a body and in turn we are all healers, caretakers of our bodies. To become aware means that you are working within the laws of the universe, there are no other laws that can be ultimately followed. This work of awareness puts the responsibility in your lap. You begin with yourself, you are the pebble that ripples out into the universe, moment-to-moment. The energy you put out into the world never goes away, it vibrates forever.

Today we are all becoming increasingly more aware. We are more aware of the effects that our human existence is having on the earth, the very thing that keeps us alive. We have damaged the earth beyond repair, and we watch as it responds. By healing ourselves we can begin to heal the earth. This work that you do on the micro level inside your body, is the very thing that will reverberate into work to be done on the macro level. The hope for our future is within each one of us.

Energy is like money—each time we use it, we lose it. Imagine you are throwing down a hundred dollar bill every time you engage in something that doesn't support your beliefs or perspectives. We wouldn't carelessly invest in something we don't need or want or that wouldn't fit into our lifestyle. The same goes for our words and actions. Being aware of our thoughts and feelings should be treated no differently. Energy, like love, compounds on itself. The more you invest in exactly what you want, the more it will manifest into your physical world.

You need to create energy as well. Look at how you nourish and support your energy and know that it is all connected (Data collecting—Research #1 Energy Input and Energy Output) And look how you use it. Money, like energy, is meant to be used. I may have energy in the bank, but is it increasing or just sitting there blocking me from my full potential?

Like everything in life, becoming more aware is a choice. We have free will, and while we may want something very badly, enjoy it even, justify it because of these very reasons, we can choose not to have it. We can acknowledge that we like it, love it even and decide not to choose it. Part of the process is getting all of yourself on board with the common goal of your chosen belief. The freedom in becoming more aware is the knowledge that you have a choice. Remember, you are the writer, director, producer and actor in your own unique production of your life.

With all your tools in hand you are now ready to live intentionally, to continue the work of creating the life you want. You are becoming more and more aware of your thoughts, feelings and emotions. You know what supports you, and what doesn't. You know what it feels like in your body, and what you want to believe about yourself and how that matches up with your vision of yourself. You're examining how it supports your mission and your values. You have created mantras to say to keep yourself alert on the road of life. Each day, each moment, are opportunities to check in, to be sure you are staying the course that you have picked for yourself. You may now even be aware that letting go was not the end of your journey but the beginning.

You are building from your experiences and the growing sense of knowing that can be clearly defined and you are filling in the gaps of your dictionary. Your job is to learn what your body is telling you, to define it accurately, so that you can trust it, all day long, in the mundane times and in the tough times.

You may be acutely aware that you are having less emotional ups and downs as you choose to conserve your energy to serve your vision. And the exciting thing is now, when something does come into your awareness, there is a vast contrast from your calm, peaceful state and the one that you just experienced. Our world is made up of so many things that we can't see with the naked eye and yet we are dramatically affected by them. Think of atoms, cells, neutrinos, viruses, bacteria, these make up most of life, in fact they rule. Our world, our universe, is filled with energy and matter, doing things that even the most knowledgeable and talented physicists look at in wonder, scratching their heads. If you are not attending to this energy, then you are missing the gunk in the corners that needs to be cleaned out in order for you to fully step into the truth. We don't have to understand it all to be open to the idea that it exists and that it can alter us.

SUMMARY

In this chapter we discussed the unseen parts of our world—spirituality and energy. In the experiments below you will be guided to expand your awareness, grow your intuition and begin the process of loving yourself and all beings in this world.

EXPERIMENT #21

EXPANDING YOUR AWARENESS

Expand your awareness to understand how our cultures have impressed and oppressed you—socioeconomic, education, racism, misogyny, anti-LGBTQ, anti-everything-different.

How has your culture confined you?

_____

_____

_____

_____

_____

_____

Expand your awareness out into the natural world. Nature is a great teacher. If an animal keeps appearing in your environment or comes to you in a dream (particularly if you don't usually see it and then all of a sudden there it is in your conscious awareness), it means something. Study the animal or insect. What are its qualities that make it unique, how does it manage its life, what are its survival skills?

What animal is coming to you lately—what animal are you noticing more of?

_____

_____

_____

_____

_____

_____

How does learning more about how this animal lives help you in your life?

_____

_____

_____

_____

_____

Take a walk into nature; a local park, hiking trail, your back-yard, or down the street. If you can't get out, look out your window into nature and observe. As you walk or observe nature, listen to your body. Hear your breath, feel your heart, and muscles and lungs. Then listen for the sounds, listen beyond the traffic and your footsteps. What do you hear? See beyond the tips of your shoes and the pavement, path, or window. Look up, look around you. What do you see? Feel beyond your body, your seat by the window, your jacket, and your clothes. Notice the breeze, the sun, touch a hanging branch, feel the high grass. What do you *feel?* Smell beyond your deodorant, lotion and shampoo. Walk up to a tree. Bend down to the grass and the dirt. What do you *smell?* Give thanks for the new sights, sounds, smells, and feelings that nature gave you. Then sit in silence.

What did you notice when you were out in nature?

_____

_____

_____

_____

_____

_____

Expand your awareness that thought energy puts everything into motion. Look around your room and begin to appreciate that every single thing is energy made into matter. Everything is vibrating energy and it began with a thought, an idea.

What have you manifested into your life?

_____

_____

_____

_____

_____

What would you like to manifest?

_____

_____

_____

_____

_____

_____

EXPERIMENT #22

TRUST YOUR INTUITION

Build your intuition by trusting it.

When you go to the grocery store, tune into what your body wants to eat. Instead of shopping from your list this time, walk slowly up and down the aisles and feel your body's energy in response to the produce, the boxes and the containers. Set your thoughts and associations aside as these were likely set up by sales and marketing. Get out of your head and into your body. Don't buy it if you don't feel high energy around it.

Notes:

_____

_____

_____

_____

_____

Go for a drive with no destination and see where you are drawn (safely) to go. Take the turn, make the stop, view the scenery, notice what is around you. Dare to get lost, trust that you won't, set aside thoughts of fear of the unknown.

Notes:

_____

_____

_____

_____

_____

Look at your long list of to-dos, shoulds, and have-tos. Consider each item, suspend your thoughts of doubts, over-whelm and opinions of failure at not getting the list done yesterday. Get out of your head and tune into what your body has energy around doing right now. And do it.

Notes:

_____

_____

_____

_____

_____

EXPERIMENT #23

LOVING KINDNESS MEDITATION

During your quiet times with yourself say the following loving kindness meditation to increase the loving connection with yourself and out into the world.

Let yourself sit in a comfortable fashion. Let your body rest and be relaxed. Let your heart be soft. Let go of any plans and preoccupations.

1. Begin with yourself. Breathe gently and recite inwardly the following traditional phrases directed to your own well-being. You begin with yourself because without loving yourself it is almost impossible to love others.

- *May I be filled with loving kindness.*
- *May I be safe from inner and outer dangers.*
- *May I be well in body and mind.*
- *May I be at ease and happy.*

As you say these phrases, imagine yourself as you are now. Adjust the words and images in any way you wish. Create the exact phrases that best open your heart of kindness. Repeat these phrases over and over again, letting the feelings permeate your body and mind. Practice this meditation for a number of weeks, until the sense of loving kindness for yourself grows.

2. When you feel you have established some stronger sense of loving kindness for yourself, you can then expand your meditation to include others. After focusing on yourself for five or 10 minutes, choose a benefactor, someone in

your life who has loved or truly cared for you. Imagine this person in your mind's eye recite the same phrases:

- *May you be filled with loving kindness.*
- *May you be safe from inner and outer dangers.*
- *May you be well in body and mind.*
- *May you be at ease and happy.*

3. Expand your meditation to include those you do not know. Imagine your neighborhood, your community, your city, your state, your country, the Earth, all of space and the stars and planets and say the phrases:

- *May you be filled with loving kindness.*
- *May you be safe from inner and outer dangers.*
- *May you be well in body and mind.*
- *May you be at ease and happy.*

MOVING ON:

You are ready to move on to the next chapter once you have completed the experiments of expanding your awareness, growing your intuition and practicing loving kindness towards yourself, your family and friends, your community and our world.

CHAPTER ELEVEN:

HOPEFULNESS AND GRATITUDE

ENERALLY, IN OUR SOCIETY WE ROOT FOR THE "WIN." WE want our teams to win, we want success, we want the speaker we are listening to to do a great job. We don't want to see failure, mess ups or adversity. We want to see the good guy win. We identify with the mistakes that others make because of our own mistakes made in our lives. But we shield ourselves from these mistakes and only focus on the successful outcome. We celebrate achievements and welcome all they represent. What we don't often realize or acknowledge is that those achievements and successes didn't likely just happen. There was intention, focus, support and effort put in over and over to attain them.

In the 60s and 70s increasing unrest grew around the Vietnam War, there were protests, new lifestyles representing free thought, challenging the establishment and the old ways of doing things. Worlds were clashing. My inner world related more to these new thoughts and ways of living and I felt my outer world clashing with them.

In the summer of 1970, when I was 10-years old, my family was on vacation and we came upon a flea market type of event where "hippies" were selling things they had made. We walked along the street from table to table, looking at them and what they had to offer for sale. I noticed and admired everything about these men and women. Their long hair, flowing skirts, halter tops, flashing smiles. They seemed to have the freedom and joy that I wanted too. I wanted so badly to stay there with them and leave my life.

Try as I might to visualize how that might even happen and how I too could have flowers in my hair, wear bell bottoms, halter tops and chokers, and live a free and joyful life, I was with my family that day. As we drove off (much too soon and without any mementos except my memories) I tried to figure out how I could get back there. As much as I wanted to just dress like these free, joyous, people I struggled with my insecurity—and likely the negative energy emanating from my mom around it. I was self-conscious but bravely wore a purple choker and braided my hair while it was wet the night before so it would frizz out boldly the next day for classes. Wearing a halter top was way out of my comfort zone as it revealed my body and I felt vulnerable. So big t-shirts, bell bottoms and long pigtails tied in thick yarn became my uniform. I found my freedom when I would go on camping trips with the Girl Scouts. Sloshing in creeks and climbing hills, standing by campfires roasting everything and poking at it with sticks. As I would gaze into the lapping flames of the campfire, the heat warming my face, surrounded by friends, I felt free. I was free to think, and smile and laugh, tell jokes and learn about my powers of building something, surviving the cold fall nights, and weathering unexpected storms. That Christmas I had asked for a pair of white go-go boots, that's all I wanted. And, I actually got them before Christmas because we were going to a family friend's house for a party and of course I realize now my mom wanted to have us all look good! I wore those go-go boots to the party and to school that winter. I would tap my toes in delight under my desk and glance down, so pleased at my gift that year.

My mom was concerned about how things looked, proper ways of doing things, saying the right things. She was focused on no conflict, put on a smile, put on your best for others. Facades. She grew up on a dusty, windy farm in western Kansas, a wheat farm with chickens in the yard until my mother's family would ring their necks, feather, cut up and fry. There's a picture of her dirty face, unkempt, windblown hair, thin gingham dress with no shoes—standing in the dirt in front of a paint-chipped step to their wood house, a washboard off to the side. Going to college at 16, she graduated from a class of five others, all of whom were mostly all relatives in her small town. Moving to the big city of Topeka was like magic for her, married to civil engineer, not a farmer, living in a house made of stone, with grass and trees. Having all the "niceties" of linens, crystal, china and silver for dinner parties, ladies' groups and church gatherings all aided her in creating the life she admired and loved.

When my parents couldn't achieve having their own children, they had to adopt a boy first and a girl second because back then families had two children and the boy was ideally the oldest. This was post-World War II. The industrial age. The boom. Success meant that families had a house, a car and two children. They had washing machines, dishwashers, gas-powered lawnmowers, coffee makers, record players and refrigerators. Trips to the beauty parlor on Fridays for parties on Saturday and church on Sunday. Every Saturday night I got a bath for the week. My mom would sit me down at her dresser mirror and take my hair and curl it into pinwheels keeping them in place with two bobby pins each. Those nights were always a bit restless as the pins would stick into my head as I tossed and turned. My hair was "straight and stringy" according to my mom. She gave me a perm when I was five-years old. Any outward flaw of mine was attended to and "fixed." Beds made, floors picked up, rooms always tidy with displays of art, candles, centerpieces, vases. On Sundays we put on our best clothes, suits and ties, dresses, slips, hose and high heels. There were expected behaviors, and rules to follow. My parents were raised this way and they raised their kids this way. I was repeating patterns of behavior that I observed all my life and I too liked nice things. All the while my inner environment was unattended, out of order, confusing—and what a mess!

One day my adult daughter made a side comment that snapped me into her perception of me. She said, "You do everything well." A wave of sadness came over me as I realized that rather than this being a compliment, it reflected a bit of jealousy, and some comparing herself to me. As you know by now, that was not my inner dialogue for most of my life. As I looked back on her life with me, now through her eyes, scenes played out of cooking and preparing food that I knew she would like, her big beaming smile with large green olives on each finger. I would keep the house picked up and cleaned, arranging toys and rooms to meet her wants and needs, painting murals with the colors and designs she wanted on her walls; a large blue bow wrapped around her closet doors matching her bedspread and eyelet-covered canopy. She watched as I prepared for the birth of her brother and painted his room with a mural of large mice playing musical instruments that matched the bedding I sewed for his crib. I took a break leaving my brush and paints for a moment and she toddled in and started painting on the walls too! I would write notes of encouragement to her, placing them inside lunches of her favorite food and a treat for school. After school we would read books, and she would dance to Barney on the coffee table in her sparkly gold shoes and princess dress. At night I would sing to her "Lullaby and Goodnight," her very own favorite bedtime song, the one I had been singing to her since the day she was born. I would sew dresses that would twirl.

As she got older and we learned in first grade that she was struggling, we took her for testing and later I took her to counseling sessions to help her manage ADHD symptoms. As her dad and I sat in parent-teacher conferences in high school I realized that they didn't care if she went to college or not. They had two tracks for kids, just make it through high school or get into college. I found a better high school for her, one that brought out her skills, talents, and gifted parts, where she fit in and could be creative and go to college. I was managing all of this as a single parent who had no emotional and financial support. She watched as I graduated with my two master's degrees and saw me apply and advance in my counseling career. She came to work after school and helped me run expressive arts groups and manage volunteers and teams. So, I guess, I started to see how she could think of me this way.

During the time of my divorce and for several years after, I continued to come to the house where the kids stayed most of the time during the week with their dad. We celebrated holidays and birthdays together throughout those years. I had an intention of co-parenting keeping my children a priority during the changes I had set into motion. I kept their lives as much the same as possible, same bedrooms, same school, same routine. I would arrive at 5 a.m. so my ex-husband could go to his job. I would clean the house, make the meals, get the kids up for school and pick them up after. I would spend the evening with them and tuck them into bed. Then I would leave, exhausted physically, emotionally, and mentally from holding everything together all day. Even in the midst of change I was trying to keep up appearances! All of my "doing" came from my love for my children and it kept me interested and creative, and it kept them happy and feeling loved and safe. It also came from my inner dialogue and a constant drive to do everything right and make everything look right.

One day as I sat playing with dolls with my daughter in her room, I heard the phone ring and heard my ex-husband greet my parents. They talked for a while and I heard him state that I was there and he asked if they would like to speak to me. They clearly said "No" as he said his goodbyes and hung up the phone. I noticed that both my daughter and I had been holding our breath, our play suspended. She had been listening too! I fought back tears, not wanting her to see that anything was wrong. Darkness surrounded me, my past closed and my future unknown. All that was available was a single pinhole and I focused on the beige carpet on my daughter's bedroom floor, dolls and clothes, and play scenarios suspended. I don't remember what happened next, but my daughter remembers that moment in time, and she is fierce in her support and alliance with me. My parents lost the love of their first grandchild that day.

Money was tight (if not nonexistent) during those first years of my divorce and I charged everything including groceries on any three of credit cards that I couldn't pay off. One month I needed just $100 to make ends meet to pay the "have to" bills. I couldn't charge these! I put a request out to the universe, and that same day I got a call from a private client who wanted to come in for a session unexpectedly. The request was fulfilled! I got to thinking that I was setting my sights a bit too narrow—it reflected my current mindset of wanting only what I needed and nothing more —it still reflected my sense of lack, not having enough and based in fear. I realized that I was asking for something outside of myself and it kept me in fear. It was too little, and often too late.

As I opened to this experience, the world I had carefully crafted began to crumble around me, again. Two months later as I was getting in my car to visit a facility that I hoped would sign up for my agency to run an art program for their families, I heard news on the radio of the plane crashing into the World Trade Center. As I arrived at the homeless shelter the television was on, and we all sat in disbelief, shock and grief as the scenes played over and over. A few weeks before September 11, my partner, my friend from church who had come out to me five years prior, said quite bluntly that she couldn't do "this" anymore. We separated, she moved out leaving everything except her clothes for me to deal with. I had a garage sale and dismantled, sold and gave away as much as I could from our lives that we had built together seeing now that none of the stuff meant anything.

I decided to go out one night when I was invited along to sing karaoke at a friend's house. I hate karaoke and had a miserable time. I arrived home around midnight, later than I wanted, and as I parked my truck and walked in, I noticed the back doors were wide open, things were in disarray, quickly left on countertops, thrown from drawers and cupboards, and the rest of what I had valued was gone. Week after week as I sat in church along with hundreds of others, I openly cried, a knot in my throat, my chest tight, tissues in my pocket. I cried for all the people lost in the plane crashes and all the people in the towers and I cried for the crashing of everything I too had built in the past five years and all that I had lost and continued to lose. I was grateful to be able to openly grieve during this time and in a strange way have my own personal grief validated by the collective grief that shook the country.

Where was hope and gratefulness in these hard times? I didn't feel like I was winning most days and I can't say that I have always kept my eye on a bright future while I was feeling defeated. And yet there are moments in time, that in contrast to the darkness, things will shine even brighter. Each disaster has the potential to break open hearts that have been hardened by life's struggles. Strangers provide support, reach out, give a hand, look outside of themselves, look around, look up and see another perspective. We find our commonalities. We're on the same road together, and what I do affects you and what you do affects me. In the end all of this is just about being responsible for the energy we put out into this world. This starts with our individual inner world.

When I turn inward, regroup, remember and claim my power and do what is right for me, I will find it. Perhaps when we are faced with adversity we work harder at this business of staying focused on what is working, what we are working for. It is in this act that we can find hope and gratefulness.

The process of self-examination is a continual, and gradual, cycle of slowly dying off, a process of discard, decay, germination, re-birth and growth, back to full bloom. We are very much of this earth and everything else on Earth follows these cycles continually without hesitation or regret. Yet, for some reason, we humans think we don't have to do this. If we take a page from nature for a moment and identify where we are in this process, we can also find hope in the process. We can find hope in that what falls away is making its way into a transformation and into something new. As we reflect on our past, instead of regret and shame at past flaws and mistakes, we can find gratitude for the increased awareness and the growth that we experience as a result and view them as universal nudges that lead us into the future with expectations of new growth. Every moment provides this opportunity. As one moment passes into the next, don't look backward, move forward. With each fall, envision winning the next time, or the next time, until you get it right. And know that we will never get it right. Let go of perfection as a goal and know that you already have everything you need. You are already who you are supposed to be. Claim your power as The One, The Only, The Best. In this knowing, you will find gratefulness and hope.

As I look out my window writing this chapter, I see the redbud tree changing from green to an ever-so-slight color of yellow and in the contrast of the mottled colors I see their shape for the first time. Every single leaf, from the biggest to the smallest, is in the shape of a heart. Love is everywhere if we will take the time to notice it. If we change our perspective.

SUMMARY

In this chapter we focused on the small moments of finding hopefulness and gratitude. In the experiments below you will be guided to reconnect with the positive parts of yourself, to strengthen your new beliefs and align your thoughts with who and what you are becoming.

EXPERIMENT #24

CHECK YOUR FOCUS

If you have gained mastery anywhere in your life, think about the effort that it took to get there. Don't dismiss even the smallest of accomplishments because of cultural norms that have confined you. If the only thing you can think of was that you finished high school, think about the hours of attending classes, taking tests and showing up even when you didn't want to, in order to get that diploma. If you can only say that you are reading this book and haven't even dressed for the day, consider the effort that went into that, finding it, purchasing it and now opening it up. Think about the neurons firing as you read it and your lungs expanding as you breathe. Look at each moment to understand that in that moment lies everything you need, rest in gratitude and thankfulness.

Accomplishment:

_____

_____

_____

What were all the smaller steps to achieve this accomplishment?

_____

_____

_____

Accomplishment:

_____

_____

_____

What were all the smaller steps to achieve this accomplishment?

_____

_____

_____

Accomplishment:

_____

_____

_____

What were all the smaller steps to achieve this accomplishment?

_____

_____

_____

EMPOWERING LANGUAGE:

The language we use comes from our thoughts and feelings and our beliefs about ourselves. Notice if you say any of these words below and start to say different words, more empowering words instead. How does it feel, does it support your new belief and perspective better?

- Replace "should" with "choose, desire, want" or "I could"
- Replace "need to" with "it's important to me to"
- Replace "have to" with "desire to"
- Replace "can't" with "I'm not willing to, I choose to"
- Replace "always, never" with "sometimes, often, seldom"
- Replace "must" with "choose, desire"
- Replace "but" with "and"
- Replace "try" with "intend, aim"
- Replace "yeah, uh-huh" with "yes"
- Replace "nah, nope, unh-unh" with "no"
- Replace "I'm just" with "I am"
- Replace "maybe" with nothing—drop it!
- Replace "I would like to," or "I want to," or "I think" with simply saying or acknowledging what you would like

or want or what you think, prefacing it diminishes your intent and calls your knowledge into doubt.

- Replace "It's not my fault" with "I am responsible for"
- Replace "It's a problem" with "It's an opportunity"
- Replace "I'm never satisfied" with "I want to learn and grow"
- Replace "Life's a struggle" with "Life's an adventure"
- Replace "I hope" with "I know"
- Replace "If only" with "next time"
- Replace "what will I do?" with "I can handle it"
- Replace "It's terrible" with "It's an opportunity to learn."

Caution * Avoid Tail enders: I graduated from high school, *but so did everyone else!* I got out of bed, *but I didn't want to.* I'm healthy, *for now!* I won, *but not by much.* Instead, I graduated from high school, I got out of bed, I'm healthy, I won.

What tailenders do you use?

Notes:

_____

_____

_____

_____

_____

EXPERIMENT #25

DEFINING WHERE YOU ARE IN THE PROCESS OF CHANGE

Moment-to-moment, in all areas, we are possibly in a different stage of change or transformation. Identify using the stages of change in the preparation chapter or the example of nature; discard, decay, where you are in your process of discard, decay, germination, re-birth and growth, to full bloom. Pull out the **Intention** that you set in chapter one before you started your work in the guidebook. Also look back in chapter two at the **Stages of Change from Collecting Data—Research # 2.**

Below reflect on where you are now in your stage of change with your Intention

Area of consideration	Stage of change	How will I move through this stage?

EXPERIMENT #26

PUTTING IT ALL TOGETHER

- Get into a routine each day.
- Breathing hourly at minimum throughout the day and when you notice an emotion rising in you.
- Catch your thoughts and listen to them. Are they tapping into a belief system that you really no longer believe?
- Tune into your body, listen to the messages it is relaying. Is it responding to emotions and thoughts—what are they?
- Correct the thoughts. Find three new perspectives and the emotions will no longer be there and the body will no longer respond in kind.
- Loosen blockages and tension in the body. Stretch, move, breath and watch your mind relax and everything shift.
- Bookend your day. Morning and evening tune into your thoughts and reflect on your day ahead and the day you completed.
- In the morning, imagine going through your day—your mind will wander. Bring it back, visualize yourself walking through your day in calm, confidence, everything going smoothly and in its perfect time. Know that when something doesn't go as you had planned that it is going exactly as needed. Look for the lesson, the reason. Wait, don't judge that experience—suspend your thoughts and emotions surrounding it.
- At the end of the day; review the day. Set up a routine in which you slowly wind down, take a shower or bath, drink tea, turn off electronics, listen to music, stretch the body.
- Experiment with what works for you and stick to it reassuring your body that you are taking care of it.

Notes:

_____

_____

_____

_____

_____

_____

_____

MOVING ON

Congratulations! You have completed the guidebook.

Throughout this book you have worked through the basics of preparing your mind, attending to your lifestyle, seeing what is and isn't working. You have put in the work of becoming more intentional and aware of your thoughts and responses. You have changed your beliefs to support what you want in life. You have seen and felt the results from your basic training of managing your energy.

It's time to move on and live your life with the experiments you have completed. Know that they will compound, and grow exponentially the more you use them. You now have more awareness of who you are, what you want and how to get there.

But you are never really *there*, there is no end to learning and discovering and creating the life you want to live.

You are ready to move on to the next step, consider learning more about Integrative Quantum Medicine tm (IQM). IQM takes you to the next level of awareness and a realization that change can be quicker. Now might be the time to continue your knowledge and work with the laws of the universe—energy. Check my website for course times or individual lessons. TheArtofLiving.com IQM Level 1 and Level 2 training.

Epilogue

TODAY, I LIVE IN MY PARENTS' HOME IN TOPEKA, KANSAS where I grew up, with my wife and daughter. We have two sibling cats,—Jack-Jack and Dash—and two dogs,—Izze an AussieLab and Seven a GoldenDoodle. My two adult children have healthy, happy, full lives of their own and we visit each other when we can. Both of my daughters are learning IQM. I spend my days teaching my clients ways they can be more mindful and in charge of their lives and several times a year I offer Level 1 and 2 IQM courses.

Both of my adopted parents and my birth mother are deceased. Two years ago, I learned that I also have a sibling two years younger than me who was also adopted. We are slowly getting to know each other and are surprised and joyful to discover our common interests and talents. I am the oldest of three siblings my birth mother had while she was single. Each of us have different unknown fathers. My youngest sibling, who is four years younger than me, was raised by my mother and committed suicide on September 24th 2007.

As I clean and purge my parents' house, I find letters and photos that speak of lives lived with grace, love, commitment and intention.

The first year in our house my mother came to me as a butterfly. She crawled onto my hand from my car and sat with me for a very long time. Through the years, as layers revealed themselves, they peeled off into acceptance, a deeper understanding, and love. My heart is filled with gratitude as I continue to be in the process of staying present, catching the small moments, focusing on the bounty of this earth and the experiences it has to offer and applying the knowledge I have shared with you in this book. I rise above it all and live and love happily.

Resources

- Biology of Belief, and Spontaneous Evolution, by Bruce Lipton
- Wheels of Life, by Anodea Judith
- You Can Heal Your Life, Louise Hay,
- Power Versus Force, by David R Hawkins,
- Animal-Speak, by Ted Andrews
- The Power of Now, by Eckhart Tolle
- The Energy Cure, by Kimberly Kingsley
- The Hidden Messages in Water, by Masuri Emoto,
- What the Bleep, The Little Book of Bleeps (as well as the movie)
- The Web That Has No Weaver, by Ted Kaptchuk
- Non-Violent Communication, by Marshall Rosenberg
- Getting to Yes, by Roger fisher, and William Ury
- A Brief History of Everything, by Ken Wilber,
- Man's Search for Meaning, by Viktor Frankl
- The Wise Heart, by Jack Kornfield

Biography

MORGAN GREY HAS BEEN a licensed clinical therapist since 1995. Morgan's formal education began with a bachelor's degree in fine arts in visual communication and illustration from the University of Kansas. She holds a master's degree in community counseling and certifications in expressive arts therapy and Integrative Quantum Medicine TM (IQM)  Practitioner and Level 1 and 2 Teacher. Morgan has developed and conducted expressive arts training curriculum and presentations for therapeutic groups, conference workshops, as well as in-services throughout her career to Arizona Children's Association, Free Arts of Arizona, Ottawa University, MHN-On Demand Workshop, Arizona Foster Care Conference, Child Abuse Prevention Conference, Arizona Group Psychotherapy,

Arizona Association for Play Therapy, Hospice Family Care to name a few. Morgan has managed and supervised individuals and teams in a variety of behavioral health settings including outpatient, shelters, group homes, residential treatment facilities, foster care and the crisis line. Today, Morgan has an online private practice, The Art of Living Studio, and provides remote counseling to individuals and couples. Throughout the year Morgan offers Level 1 and 2 IQM intensives and continues to write interactive and inspiring workbooks for others to continue in their growth.